THE 100+ SERIES™

GRAMMAR

Essential Practice for Key Grammar Topics

Grades 7–8

D1306748

Carson-Dellosa Publishing, LLC
Greensboro, North Carolina

Credits

Content Editor: Sara H. Blackwood

Visit *carsondellosa.com* for correlations to Common Core, state, national, and Canadian provincial standards.

Carson-Dellosa Publishing, LLC
PO Box 35665
Greensboro, NC 27425 USA
carsondellosa.com

ISBN 978-1-4838-1558-9
01-033057784

Table of Contents

Common Core Alignment Chart

Common Core State Standard*		Practice Page(s)
Language Standards		
Conventions of Standard English	7.L.1–7.L.2	1–91
Knowledge of Language	7.L.3	5–7, 23, 30, 32–37, 39–43, 45–48, 53, 57, 58, 63, 65, 66, 68–71, 73, 78, 82–84, 87–89, 91–99
Vocabulary Acquisition and Use	7.L.4, –7.L.6	94–101, 119, 120
Conventions of Standard English	8.L.1–8.L.2	102–118
Knowledge of Language	8.L.3	108–112,
Vocabulary Acquisition and Use	8.L.4–8.L.6	94–101, 119, 120

* © Copyright 2010. National Governors Association Center for Best Practices and Council of Chief State School Officers. All rights reserved.

Introduction

Good grammar skills are essential for effective writing and communication. Organized by specific grammar rules, this book will enhance students' knowledge and usage of proper grammar. These skills include the basic parts of speech, sentence components, vocabulary, and other conventions of Standard English.

The grade-appropriate exercises in this series will strengthen any language arts program. Students will practice various grammar skills and concepts are practiced and reviewed throughout the book through activities that align to the Common Core State Standards in English language arts. The standards and corresponding pages are listed in the Common Core Alignment Chart above. Use this chart to plan your instruction, for skill practice, or for remediation of a specific standard.

Capitalization

The words *north, south, east,* and *west* are not capitalized when they refer to directions. They are capitalized when they refer to specific areas of the country.

Henry traveled <u>east</u> to see his sister.

Henry traveled to the <u>East Coast</u> to see his mother.

The names given to planets and stars are capitalized, but words like *planet, sun, moon,* and *star* are not capitalized.

The pieces of the comet bombarded <u>Jupiter</u>.

The <u>moon</u> rose in the night sky.

The words derived from proper nouns are usually capitalized.

The <u>Egyptian</u> tourists started snapping pictures.

Names of deities and sacred books are capitalized.

<u>Jehova</u>, the *Koran*

Circle the words that should be capitalized.

1. we live east of the river.

2. living in the midwest gives one a different view of the world.

3. the two scientists disagreed about the impact of the comet.

4. if you drive far enough north, you will avoid the traffic jams.

5. yolanda likes to watch the latin american dances.

6. some people had a hard time realizing that the south had lost the war.

7. there is a passage in the bible which talks about forgiveness.

8. the boy studied the talmud.

Use the words to write sentences that are correctly punctuated and capitalized.

9. german _____

10. elizabethan theater _____

11. venus _____

12. the mideast _____

13. the south _____

More Capitalization

Capitalize special titles when they precede a person's name.

  You would never guess that <u>Doctor</u> Gregory is a brain surgeon.

Capitalize geographic names.

  Our family made the drive up <u>Pikes Peak</u>.

Capitalize the names of streets, bridges, dams, hotels, monuments, parks, etc.

  My brother was in a demonstration in <u>Grant Park</u>.

Capitalize the names of historical periods, historical events, and historical documents.

  We just finished studying the <u>French Revolution</u>.

Capitalize the names of government bodies and departments.

  The <u>United Nations</u> approved the policy unanimously.

Circle the words that should be capitalized.

1. Have you ever sailed on the red sea?

2. The battle of midway was a turning point in world war II.

3. The bill sponsored by senator javits was defeated.

4. big ben, a clock tower in london, is one of the most well-known landmarks in the world.

5. He was elected to parliament.

6. The senators walked toward the white house.

7. Maybe we could get that information from the associated press.

Use the words to write sentences that are correctly punctuated and capitalized.

8. the taj mahal _____

9. the bering strait _____

10. mount everest _____

11. the battle of waterloo _____

More Capitalization

Capitalize the main words in titles of books, movies, magazines, songs, etc. Don't capitalize prepositions, coordinating conjunctions, or articles unless they are the first or last words of the title.

Pride and Prejudice is my favorite book.

Do not capitalize the names of school subjects unless they are languages or unless they are followed by a number indicating a specific course.

Wally is taking <u>English</u> and <u>biology</u> this term.

All freshmen must take <u>Algebra 101</u>.

Capitalize words that show family relationship when they are used as a name or part of a name.

My <u>Uncle Don</u> has the greatest sense of humor.→ *Some grammarians say: Do NOT capitalize a family relationship if a personal pronoun comes ahead of it.*

Does your <u>uncle</u> have a sense of humor?

↳ *My uncle Don has the greatest sense of humor.*

1. Circle the words that should be capitalized.

my mom	aunt sarah	*good housekeeping*
grandmothers	grandma	"the drummer boy of shiloh"
english	history	the oxford english dictionary
chemistry 101	your cousin	"stopping by woods on a snowy evening"
dad	uncle umberto	much ado about nothing

Use the words to write sentences that are correctly punctuated and capitalized.

2. aunt gertrude _____

3. cousin _____

4. french _____

5. "hey jude" _____

6. *vogue* magazine _____

7. biology 344 _____

8. *the great gatsby* _____

Recognizing Nouns

Nouns are words that name persons, places, things, or ideas. Nouns identify (That person is <u>John</u>. That place is <u>home</u>. That thing is a <u>ball</u>. That idea is <u>responsibility</u>).

kite, president, bell, book, candle, freedom, ships, shoes, democracy, Mongolia, doctor, house, park

Write whether each noun describes a **person**, **place**, **thing**, or **idea**.

1. rock	5. Leo Valdez	9. tree	13. happiness
2. firefighter	6. jet	10. rage	14. Uruguay
3. China	7. Michigan	11. Rachel	15. joy
4. book	8. pen	12. boat	16. emotion

The words *a*, *an*, and *the* are often used before nouns. These words are known as **articles**. If a noun begins with a consonant sound, use the article *a*. If a noun begins with a vowel sound, use the article *an*.

Write the correct article (**a** or **an**) to go with each nouns. Remember: it is the sound, not the spelling, which helps you make this determination.

17. _____ book	21. _____ tiger	25. _____ exclamation
18. _____ hour	22. _____ penguin	26. _____ president
19. _____ classroom	23. _____ sea	27. _____ idea
20. _____ eagle	24. _____ keyboard	28. _____ opera

29. On another sheet of paper, write a short paragraph about an issue that is in the news. Underline each noun that you use.

Common and Proper Nouns

Proper nouns are the names of specific persons, places, or things. They are spelled with capital letters. Your name is a proper noun.

London, Usain Bolt, Florence Nightingale, Taj Mahal

All other nouns are called **common nouns**. Common nouns do not name specific persons, places, or things.

city, athlete, nurse, building

If the word listed below is a proper noun, write the common noun that describes it. If it is a common noun, give an example of a proper noun that matches the word. Circle the proper noun in each pair of words.

1. car _____

2. teacher _____

3. Sherlock Holmes _____

4. *Sputnik* _____

5. country _____

6. Michael _____

7. girl _____

8. Pacific Ocean _____

9. Cleopatra _____

10. actress _____

11. Mark Twain _____

12. constellation _____

13. Buddhism _____

14. Mount Everest _____

15. Sydney _____

16. *Things Fall Apart* _____

17. Choose five sets of nouns above. For each pair of words, write one sentence that uses both the proper and common noun correctly.

_____

_____

_____

_____

_____

_____

Concrete and Abstract Nouns

A **concrete noun** names something that can be seen or touched.
    bridge, shell, car

An **abstract noun** names an idea, quality, or state of mind.
    liberty, intelligence, happiness

Label each noun as concrete (**C**) or abstract (**A**).

_____ 1. fence

_____ 2. success

_____ 3. Dr. Xiang

_____ 4. sadness

_____ 5. research

_____ 6. desk

_____ 7. Pecos River

_____ 8. hat

_____ 9. walnuts

_____ 10. imagination

_____ 11. forgetfulness

_____ 12. telephone

Circle each concrete noun and underline each abstract noun.

13. Mount Everest, located in Tibet, is the highest mountain on Earth.

14. Tibetan nomads must exert a lot of energy in their daily struggle to live.

15. One skill they possess is horsemanship.

16. Becoming a Buddhist monk is considered a high honor among the Tibetan people.

17. The Dalai Lama, Tibet's leader, is considered an inspiration to his people.

18. Tibet has far fewer monasteries today than it did in the past.

19. The monks in the monasteries encourage art, education, and worship.

List three abstract nouns and three concrete nouns.

20. (abstract) _____   (concrete) _____

    (abstract) _____   (concrete) _____

    (abstract) _____   (concrete) _____

Plural Nouns

Plural means more than one. The plural of most nouns is formed by adding *–s*.
> book, books; time, times; house, houses; lesson, lessons

If a noun ends in *s, x, ch, z, sh*, or *ss*, add *–es*.
> bus, buses; fox, foxes; lunch, lunches; waltz, waltzes; dish, dishes; boss, bosses

Write sentences using the plural forms of the nouns listed.

1. pilot, airplane

    _____

2. box, square

    _____

3. team, bus

    _____

4. boss, job

    _____

5. window, tree

    _____

6. book, class

    _____

7. batter, hit

    _____

8. cloud, wish

    _____

9. lesson, suffix

    _____

10. branch, root

    _____

Write two sentences that include at least one singular noun and one plural noun.
Underline the singular nouns and circle the plural nouns.

11. _____

12. _____

More Plural Nouns

To form the plural of nouns that end with *y* preceded by a consonant, change the *y* to an *i* and add *–es.*

    baby, babies

For nouns that end with *y* preceded by a vowel, just add *–s.*

    key, keys

To form the plural of a word that ends in an *o* preceded by a vowel, add *–s.* For words that end in an *o* preceded by a consonant, you usually add *–es.* (Check a dictionary if you're unsure.)

    folio, folios; tomato, tomatoes

For words that end in *f* or *fe*, sometimes change the *f* to *v* and add *–es*; other times, just add *–s.* (Check a dictionary if you're unsure.)

    knife, knives; safe, safes; chief, chiefs

Write the plural form next to each singular noun.

1. monkey _____
2. class _____
3. tax _____
4. berry _____
5. loaf _____
6. latch _____
7. fez _____
8. wish _____
9. hoof _____
10. galley _____

11. horse _____
12. roof _____
13. puff _____
14. honey _____
15. color _____
16. waltz _____
17. wife _____
18. victory _____
19. potato _____
20. tress _____

Some words don't follow any rules—their plurals have to be learned. Check a dictionary and write the plural form for each noun.

21. crisis _____
22. brother-in-law _____
23. man _____

24. ox _____
25. spoonful _____
26. datum _____

Possessive Nouns

Nouns that show ownership are called **possessive nouns**.

To form the possessive of a singular noun, add an apostrophe and an *s* (*–'s*).

Tom's bell, the <u>author's</u> book, <u>society's</u> values

To form the possessive of a plural noun, only add an apostrophe if the word ends in *s*.

the <u>authors'</u> books, the <u>Nortons'</u> home

If the plural of the noun does not end in s, add an apostrophe and an *s* (*–'s*).

<u>men's</u> race, <u>children's</u> hour

Write the possessive form of each noun.

1. woman _____
2. mice _____
3. horses _____
4. girls _____
5. teacher _____
6. umbrella _____
7. princess _____
8. home _____
9. players _____
10. students _____
11. host _____

12. presidents _____
13. scissors _____
14. Schindler _____
15. leaves _____
16. witnesses _____
17. actress _____
18. statue _____
19. pants _____
20. river _____
21. company _____
22. nurse _____

Write a short paragraph describing some of your and your family's favorite possessions. Underline the possessive nouns.

_____

_____

_____

_____

_____

Collective Nouns

A **collective noun** names a group of persons, places, or things.

    band, team, audience, New Zealand

When a collective noun refers to the group as a unit, the noun is considered singular.

    The <u>family</u> went on vacation.

    The <u>flock</u> headed on its northern course.

When a collective noun refers to the individual members of the group who are acting separately, the noun is considered plural.

    The <u>class</u> brought their pets to show and tell.

    The <u>family</u> are all going their separate ways.

Indicate whether the collective nouns in the following sentences are singular (**S**) or plural (**P**). Circle the correct word if there is a choice to be made.

_____ 1.   The jury filed out of the courtroom.

_____ 2.   The family (is, are) going on vacation to Georgia.

_____ 3.   During the game, the crowd (was, were) very enthusiastic.

_____ 4.   The team (is, are) getting on the bus after (its, their) heartbreaking loss.

_____ 5.   The school staff worked throughout the summer on (its, their) lesson plans.

_____ 6.   That group of spectators (is, are) getting awfully rowdy.

_____ 7.   The symphony (is, are) playing some of the old favorites.

_____ 8.   The set of books fell from the shelf.

_____ 9.   The audience (is, are) returning to (its, their) cars.

_____ 10. The staff (was, were) very happy about (its, their) bonuses.

Write a short paragraph using at least three collective nouns. Write **S** or **P** above each collective noun to show if it is singular or plural.

_____

_____

_____

_____

Name_____

Predicate Nouns

A **predicate noun** is a noun used as a subject complement. Predicate nouns follow linking verbs.

Theodore Roosevelt was the <u>president</u> back then.

Circle the linking verb and underline the predicate noun.

1. After his retirement, Macon became a consultant.

2. Uncle Emmett was the best storyteller in the family.

3. Becca is a talented student.

4. Rashawnda was president of the club last year.

5. Sucre is the capital of Bolivia.

6. "The Raven" is the most popular poem in the anthology.

7. Marcella became an authority on fungi.

8. The president is the commander in chief.

9. Switzerland became a member of the United Nations in 2002.

10. Mischa was a talented sculptor.

11. Grandfather became a carpenter.

12. The principal is chairperson of the committee.

13. The general was the leader of the army.

14. The boy was a soldier in the war.

Write four sentences using predicate nouns. Circle the predicate nouns.

15. _____

16. _____

17. _____

18. _____

Persons of Pronouns

The **person** of a pronoun tells whether the pronoun being used is the speaker, the one spoken to, or the one spoken about.

> The **first person** refers to the speaker.
> I am speaking.
>
> The **second person** refers to the one spoken to.
> You are the one.
>
> The **third person** refers to the person or thing spoken about.
> She/It is beautiful.

Identify the person of each underlined pronoun by writing **1**, **2**, or **3** in the parentheses at the end of each sentence.

1. He was a soldier in World War I. (   )

2. I would like you to study the chapter on the causes of the war. (   )

3. We must understand the problems left behind at the end of the war. (   )

4. The leader of the country guided it through a very difficult time. (   )

5. I admire Napoleon. (   )

6. He was a talented leader. (   )

7. The war created many problems, but it also solved some serious disputes. (   )

8. Have you studied this war before? (   )

9. My history teacher was correct when she said this material was important to learn. (   )

10. We will soon learn a poem written during this time. (   )

Write one sentence using first person, one sentence using second person, and one using third person. Circle the pronouns which indicate the person.

11. (first person) _____

12. (second person) _____

13. (third person) _____

Personal Pronouns

A **pronoun** is a word that takes the place of a noun. A **personal pronoun** indicates the speaker (first person), the one spoken to (second person), or the one spoken about (third person).

   First person pronouns: I, my, mine, me, we, our, ours, us

   Second person pronouns: you, your, yours

   Third person pronouns: he, she, it, his, her, hers, its, him, her, they, their, theirs, them

Write **1** above first person pronouns, **2** above second person pronouns, and **3** above third person pronouns.

1. We are going to study the life of Joan of Arc.

2. What do you think we will learn from this study?

3. When Joan of Arc was thirteen years old, she realized her life was going to change.

4. She became convinced that Charles VII, the King of France, needed her help to drive out the English soldiers.

5. If you had been there, you might have doubted Joan's ability to help.

6. When she was 17, she finally talked to the king.

7. Joan had talked to a commander first, but he laughed at her.

8. They did not think she would be of any help.

9. She led them in battle and was victorious at the Battle of Orleans.

10. Eventually, she was captured and held prisoner by the English.

11. They thought she was a witch and burned her at the stake on May 30, 1431.

12. We will probably never know all of the details of her exciting life.

Write three sentences about a daring adventure on which you would like to embark. Use at least one personal pronoun in each sentence. Underline the personal pronouns.

13. _____

14. _____

15. _____

Indefinite Pronouns

An **indefinite pronoun** is one which refers generally, not specifically, to places or things. Some indefinite pronouns are always singular, some are always plural, and some may be either singular or plural.

Singular indefinite pronouns: anybody, anyone, another, each, either, everybody, everyone, nobody, no one, neither, one, other, someone, somebody, everything, anything, something

Plural indefinite pronouns: many, both, few, several, others

Indefinite pronouns that may be either singular or plural: all, any, most, some, none

Some indefinite pronouns may be singular or plural. These are the only indefinite pronouns that are affected by phrases or clauses separating them from the verb.

Circle the verb or helping verb that agrees in number with the indefinite pronoun subject.

1. Many of the students (like, likes) to be challenged.

2. Some of the material in this book (is, are) interesting.

3. Either of the two sisters (is, are) willing to pay for the gift.

4. Many of the people (was, were) disgusted with the media coverage.

5. Neither of the two teams (deserve, deserves) to play in the finals.

6. Anyone who thinks they know the answer (has, have) to raise his or her hand.

7. Each of the monkeys in the cage (play, plays) to the audience.

8. Most of the rocks in the bag (is, are) worthless.

9. All of the fish in the creek (was, were) killed by the insecticide.

10. Everyone who is interested (is, are) welcome to sign up.

11. Everybody in the band (is, are) very talented.

12. All of us (wish, wishes) the best for your future.

13. Several of the women on the job site (was, were) given a raise.

14. Few teachers (has, have) been as energetic as she has been.

15. One elephant (has, have) done a tremendous amount of damage to the village.

Possessive and Interrogative Pronouns

A **possessive pronoun** is one that indicates ownership or possession.
  Possessive pronouns: my, mine, your, yours, his, her, hers, its, our, ours, their, theirs

Circle each possessive pronoun.

1. Her vacation was planned a long time in advance.

2. My travel agent helped put together her itinerary.

3. His office telephoned many hotels and motels around the country.

4. He was asking about their best rate.

5. One hotel sent a brochure of its services.

6. He drove their van to the airport.

7. Our airport is open all night.

8. Is that suitcase hers?

9. Those boxes are theirs.

10. Our flight is delayed.

An **interrogative pronoun** introduces a question.
  Interrogative pronouns: who, whom, whose, what, which

Circle each interrogative pronoun.

11. Who will win this game tonight?

12. Which is your house?

13. What are we having for dinner?

14. To whom will the people of this country turn?

15. Whose child is this?

Use interrogative pronouns to write two sentences of your own.

16. what _____

17. which _____

Reflexive and Relative Pronouns

Reflexive pronouns are formed by adding *-self* or *-selves* to certain forms of personal pronouns.

   First person reflexive pronouns: myself, ourselves

   Second person reflexive pronouns: yourself, yourselves

   Third person reflexive pronouns: himself, herself, itself, themselves

Circle each reflexive pronoun.

1. I will use all of my efforts to develop myself to the best of my ability.

2. Have you done all of the problems by yourself?

3. John prepared the meat by himself.

4. We must defend ourselves because no one else will.

5. You might find yourselves needing help one day.

6. Rachel knew herself well enough to know when to ask for help.

7. She watched herself on TV and felt foolish.

Relative pronouns are used to introduce groups of words that act as adjectives.

   Relative pronouns: who, whose, whom, which, that

Circle each relative pronoun and underline the group of words it introduces.

8. A breakfast that includes fruit is often recommended by nutritionists.

9. People who eat a good breakfast are full of energy in the late morning hours.

10. The dietician whom I have put my trust in is planning my meals.

11. She showed me a low-fat diet that I must follow.

12. She is a person who always eats healthy foods.

13. The diet, which I started last night, is easy to follow.

14. My sister, who is very slender, can eat whatever she wants.

15. She can't understand a person like me who has to watch everything I eat.

Number and Gender of Pronouns

A pronoun must agree with its antecedent (the noun it refers to) in **number** and **gender**. If the noun is singular, the pronoun must be singular. If the noun is plural, the pronoun must be plural. If the noun is masculine, the pronoun must be masculine. If the noun is feminine, the pronoun must be feminine. If the noun is neuter (neither gender indicated), the pronoun must also be neuter.

Write **S** under the pronouns that are singular and **P** under those that are plural. Write **F** above the pronouns that are female, **M** above those that are male, and **N** above those that are neuter.

1. Nora is the first person I would invite to the party. She is fun to talk to.

2. The car veered to the left of the line. It then stopped suddenly.

3. Can you go to the mall with Sara and me? We are leaving at 1:00 pm.

4. We slid down the waterslide. It was a very fast ride.

5. Juan's idea of a good time is to sit in front of the TV all night. He doesn't even like to play basketball.

6. We saw the plane heading toward the airport. Dad and I both checked the time to see if it was late.

7. The pilot let Bill sit in the cockpit. Boy, was he thrilled!

8. Have you ever flown on a plane? Would you like to fly?

Write a pronoun to take the place of each noun.

9. shelter _____

10. soccer _____

11. relatives _____

12. men _____

13. dolphins_____

14. mountain _____

15. bull _____

16. daffodils _____

17. trains _____

18. ewe _____

Recognizing Verbs

A **verb** is a word that expresses action (action verbs) or a state of being (linking verbs).
action: run, fish, swim, travel, stumble   **state of being**: looks, is, were, seems

Circle each verb and indicate whether it is an action verb (**A**) or a linking verb (**L**).

_____ 1. Powerful telescopes probe the remote reaches of the universe.

_____ 2. New technology strips away old limitations.

_____ 3. Computers adjust the optics.

_____ 4. Hawaii's Keck Telescope is amazing.

_____ 5. The Milky Way is an example of a spiral galaxy.

_____ 6. The Milky Way contains hundreds of billions of stars.

_____ 7. A supernova is an exploding star.

_____ 8. A lot of information about the galaxy is yet to be learned.

Identify each verb as an action verb (**A**) or a linking verb (**L**).

_____ 9. hugs the child   _____ 13. am sorry   _____ 17. read a book

_____ 10. was a pilot   _____ 14. lifted the bar   _____ 18. sings the song

_____ 11. threw the ball   _____ 15. seems cold   _____ 19. looks pretty

_____ 12. baked a cake   _____ 16. mail the letter   _____ 20. is happy

Write two sentences that contain action verbs and two that contain state of being verbs.
Underline the action verbs once and circle the state of being verbs.

21. (action) _____

22. (action) _____

23. (action) _____

24. (being) _____

25. (being) _____

26. (being) _____

More Verbs

Circle each verb and tell if it is an action verb (**A**) or a linking verb (**L**).

_____ 1. Macaws are the largest of all parrots.

_____ 2. Their very long tails are unique in the parrot family.

_____ 3. Their wings are long and pointed.

_____ 4. Macaws eat fruit, nuts, and seeds.

_____ 5. The macaw screams loudly.

_____ 6. The macaw's coloring is spectacular.

_____ 7. The scarlet macaw is the best known species.

_____ 8. Eighteen species of these parrots live in South America.

_____ 9. These birds are often poached.

_____ 10. People easily tame macaws.

_____ 11. Macaws' big beaks are extremely powerful.

_____ 12. The birds fly swiftly over the rain forest.

_____ 13. These large parrots nest in the holes of trees.

_____ 14. They are not common household pets.

_____ 15. Macaws live in forested areas.

Write a short paragraph about a pet you would like to have. Include both action and linking verbs. Circle all of the verbs.

_____

_____

_____

_____

_____

Name_____

Regular Verbs

A **regular verb** is one which forms its past tense and past participle by adding *-d* or *-ed* to the present tense form.

walk, walked, (have/has/had) walked

fix, fixed, (have/has/had) fixed

call, called, (have/has/had) called

Write the past and the past participle forms of the verbs.

Present	Past		Past Participle
1. crawl	_____	(have/has/had)	_____
2. skate	_____	(have/has/had)	_____
3. fish	_____	(have/has/had)	_____
4. climb	_____	(have/has/had)	_____
5. love	_____	(have/has/had)	_____
6. answer	_____	(have/has/had)	_____
7. travel	_____	(have/has/had)	_____
8. contend	_____	(have/has/had)	_____
9. pretend	_____	(have/has/had)	_____
10. develop	_____	(have/has/had)	_____

Use each verb in a sentence.

11. derived _____

12. has commanded _____

13. have served _____

14. opened _____

15. has watched _____

16. have crashed _____

17. jumped _____

Irregular Verbs

An **irregular verb** is one that does not form its past tense and past participle by adding -d or -ed to the present tense form

    begin, began, (have/has/had) begun

    lead, led, (have/has/had) led

    grow, grew, (have/has/had) grown

Write the past and past participle form of each verb.

Present	Past		Past Participle
1. freeze	_____	(have/has/had)	_____
2. break	_____	(have/has/had)	_____
3. fight	_____	(have/has/had)	_____
4. become	_____	(have/has/had)	_____
5. see	_____	(have/has/had)	_____
6. shake	_____	(have/has/had)	_____
7. give	_____	(have/has/had)	_____
8. eat	_____	(have/has/had)	_____
9. take	_____	(have/has/had)	_____
10. wear	_____	(have/has/had)	_____

Use each verb to write a sentence. Underline each present tense verb once, each past tense verb twice, and each past participle verb three times.

11. drew _____

12. have gone _____

13. has frozen _____

14. creeps _____

15. fell _____

16. has bitten _____

Linking Verbs

A **linking verb** does not show action. It connects a word or words in the predicate to the subject in the sentence. Some very common linking verbs are forms of *be*: am, are, is, was, were.

Father <u>is</u> a banker.   I <u>am</u> a student.

Underline each linking verb and circle the two words that are joined by it.

1.   Water is part of all living things.

2.   Water molecules are simple in structure.

3.   Water management is a complex problem.

4.   A desert is a hot, barren region.

5.   Desert living is common.

6.   Farming is restricted.

7.   Rainfall is scarce.

8.   Water for cities is sometimes difficult to find.

9.   States which lack water supplies are often desperate for help.

10.   Nearby rivers are sources of water.

11.   It is important to consider the ecological effects of any diversion of water.

12.   Some desert areas are cold.

13.   Most deserts are very hot.

14.   The largest desert is the Sahara.

Write four sentences about the geography of your hometown using linking verbs.

15.   _____

16.   _____

17.   _____

18.   _____

More Linking Verbs

Forms of *be* are common linking verbs. Other linking verbs include g*row, look, became, appear, look, taste,* and *remain*.

Note: A verb is being used as a linking verb if you can substitute the verb *is* or *was* for it.

The food <u>tasted</u> spicy.   The food <u>was</u> spicy.

Underline each linking verb and circle the two words that are joined by it.

1. A mountain lion remains a common sight in some parts of South America.

2. The puma is a mountain lion.

3. The lioness walking through the grass looked powerful.

4. When people approach, the puma becomes secretive.

5. To some ranchers, the panther became a nuisance.

6. Their extinction seemed possible.

7. Environmentalists became interested in their plight.

8. The puma is a territorial animal.

9. This information became crucial to help save the animal.

10. Today, the puma is plentiful again.

Write sentences using the linking verbs listed below. Remember to test your verb choice by seeing if you can substitute *is* or *was* for the linking verb.

11. grow _____

12. has felt _____

13. seems _____

14. tasted _____

15. has remained _____

16. was _____

Transitive Verbs

A **transitive verb** is an action verb that is followed by a direct object. The verb "transmits" the action from the subject to the object.

The (teacher) graded three (papers).

Underline each transitive verb and circle each subject and direct object.

1. The fire cast dancing shadows across the room.

2. The choir bought new outfits for the concert.

3. The sleigh rails hit the roof with a loud bang.

4. Roberto handled the flaming torch with ease.

5. The disc jockey picked a song from the list.

6. The outfielder hit the wall with a thud.

7. The goalie stopped the ball.

8. The horse jumped the obstacle with ease.

9. Kenyon slugged the baseball into the outfield.

10. He served the tennis ball over the net.

11. The woman painted the room.

12. Chrissie washed the windows.

13. My friend types 80 words per minute.

14. The toddler slammed the cupboard drawer on his fingers.

Write four sentences about a party. Be sure to use transitive verbs. Underline the transitive verbs and circle the direct objects.

15. _____

16. _____

17. _____

18. _____

Intransitive Verbs

An **intransitive verb** does not need an object to complete its meaning. It is frequently followed by a prepositional phrase.

The tower <u>collapsed</u> to the ground.

Underline each intransitive verb and circle each subject.

1. The city of Jerusalem is located near the center of Israel.

2. The control of the city of Jerusalem has changed often over the centuries.

3. The city was captured by King David.

4. Under his rule, the city flourished.

5. However, it was sacked by the Babylonians in 587 or 586 BC.

6. The great Temple of Jerusalem was built by King Solomon.

7. The Temple was destroyed.

8. Jewish people gather every day at the Wailing Wall.

9. A mosque, the Dome of the Rock, was built on the same site.

10. A holy place called the Church of the Holy Sepulcher, stands on a site nearby.

11. Jerusalem is revered by Jews, Christians, and Muslims.

12. Throughout history, tensions have arisen between the groups.

13. Many plans for resolving the disputes have failed.

14. All signs in the city are printed in three languages—Hebrew, Arabic, and English.

15. Pilgrims come from all over the world to Jerusalem.

Write four sentences about your city or one that you have visited. Include an intransitive verb in each sentence. Underline the intransitive verbs and circle the subjects.

16. _____

17. _____

18. _____

19. _____

Simple Tenses

The tense of a verb indicates when an action takes place. **Present tense** indicates action or being that is happening now.

Susan <u>loves</u> ice cream. She <u>is</u> here.

Past tense indicates action or being that was completed in the past.

Matthew <u>loved</u> the new movie. He <u>was</u> here.

Future tense indicates action or being that will take place in the future. The auxiliary verbs *will* and *shall* are used with the principal verb to form the future tense.

Ellen <u>will love</u> this house. She <u>will be</u> here tomorrow.

Label each verb as present tense (**P**), past tense (**PA**), or future tense (**F**). Then, rewrite the sentence using another tense.

_____ 1. I will hike to the top of the mountain.

_____

_____ 2. He fought against the onslaught of mosquitoes.

_____

_____ 3. Daniel compared this trip to others.

_____

_____ 4. They wear all the standard gear.

_____

_____ 5. We shall elect a leader!

_____

_____ 6. She was an excellent survivalist.

_____

Write one sentence in each simple tense about a camping trip.

7. present _____

8. past _____

9. future _____

Verb Phrases

A **verb phrase** is a group of words that does the work of a single verb. The phrase includes one principal verb and one or more helping verbs.

The teacher <u>was trying</u> to control the class.

Underline each verb phrase and circle the helping verbs.

1. Charles Darwin was born in 1809.

2. He was raised in Shrewsbury, England.

3. The theory of evolution was introduced by Charles Darwin in the 1850s.

4. Many people are attracted by the logic of the theory.

5. The theory has been refined over the years.

6. Darwin was exploring on the *HMS Beagle* in 1831.

7. He had studied plant and animal life on his travels.

8. He was forming an explanation for the phenomena he observed.

9. His theory was supported by Alfred Russell Wallace, a noted British scientist.

10. Darwin was convinced that modern species evolved from earlier ones.

11. He was fascinated by the process of natural selection.

12. His place in history was strengthened by his book, *The Origin of Species*.

13. Darwin's work has had influence on religious thought.

14. Many people have opposed his theories.

15. Other writers and scientists have referred to Darwin's ideas in their own work.

Write four sentences about geography which contain verb phrases. Underline the verb phrases and circle the helping verbs.

16. _____

17. _____

18. _____

19. _____

Identifying Adjectives

An **adjective** modifies a noun or pronoun. It gives specific information by telling *what kind, how many,* or *which one.*

green grass, two swimmers, this book

Underline each adjective. Then, tell what question it answers by writing **1** (what kind?), **2** (how many?), or **3** (which one?) above it.

1. Raul took his mangy, old dog for a long walk.

2. The dog, Joshua, rose from the warm bricks in front of the blazing hearth.

3. He did not understand why anyone would venture out into the cold weather.

4. Raul wore his bright red stocking cap pulled tightly over his big ears.

5. The cold air stung his red nose as he slogged through the blinding snow.

6. Those majestic pines were covered with a heavy layer of snow.

7. Joshua immediately had tiny icicles form in the fur of his four paws.

8. He stopped two times to try to remove the icy buildup.

9. When Ralph saw the pitiful look on Joshua's face, he knew he had made a mistake.

10. The dog endured the bitter wind.

11. He turned back to the warm house they had just left.

12. Joshua raced ahead to get back to the safe haven of his peaceful, toasty hearth.

13. Ralph peeled off the several layers of thick wool clothes and sat by the roaring fire.

14. He decided that the next time he took a long walk, it would be a warm, spring day.

15. The faithful dog wagged his bushy tail.

Write three sentences about a summer day using at least one adjective in each. Underline the adjectives.

16. _____

17. _____

18. _____

Descriptive Adjectives

A **descriptive adjective** describes a noun or a pronoun. It indicates a quality or condition of a noun.

   dark coat, clear stream, mild cold

Underline the descriptive adjective(s) in each sentence.

1. The dinosaurs were the dominant land animal 65 million years ago.

2. The name was derived from a Greek word meaning "terrible lizard."

3. These animals reached gigantic proportions.

4. A large number of dinosaurs were flesh eaters.

5. Some dinosaurs abandoned this diet for a herbivorous diet.

6. The earlier and more primitive types were actually small, reptile-like animals.

7. Suddenly, the record of the huge monsters stops.

8. How do we explain this sudden extinction?

9. One theory blames temperature changes.

10. Another theory suggests that geological changes occurred which reduced food sources.

11. Many thrilling movies revolve around these amazing reptiles.

12. Kids all over the world would miss hearing blood-curdling screams in their favorite dinosaur movies.

Write five sentences about dinosaurs using at least one descriptive adjective in each. Underline the descriptive adjectives.

13. _____

14. _____

15. _____

16. _____

17. _____

Comparative Degree of Adjectives

The **comparative degree** of an adjective is used when comparing two persons or things. It shows a greater or lesser degree of quality.

Almost every one-syllable adjective forms its comparative degree by adding -er.

> strong<u>er</u>, neat<u>er</u>, warm<u>er</u>

An adjective with two or more syllables forms its comparative degree by adding *more* or *less* in front of the adjective.

> <u>more</u> clever, <u>less</u> difficult

An adjective that ends in *y* usually forms its comparative degree by changing the *y* to *i* and adding -er.

> hand<u>ier</u>, clums<u>ier</u>

Underline each adjective that is in the comparative degree.

1. It was a stormier night than usual at our cottage.

2. First there was a harder rain than we were used to seeing.

3. This was followed by stronger winds than we experience at home.

4. If the roof had been flimsier, it would have blown away.

5. But the roof was more sturdy than we thought.

6. I can't imagine a more dismal evening.

7. Large hailstones started to fall, followed by even larger ones.

8. My sister, who is younger than I am, was scared.

9. We heard a clap of thunder which was louder than an explosion.

10. The next day brought a calmer sky.

Write four sentences using at least one adjective in the comparative degree in each. Underline the comparative adjectives.

11. _____

12. _____

13. _____

14. _____

Superlative Degree of Adjectives

The **superlative degree** of an adjective is used when more than two persons or things are being compared. It indicates that a quality is possessed to the greatest or least degree by one of the persons or things being compared.

Adjectives with one syllable usually form the superlative degree by adding -est.

strong<u>est</u>, neat<u>est</u>, warm<u>est</u>

An adjective with two or more syllables forms the superlative degree by adding *most* or *least* in front of the adjective.

<u>most</u> clever, <u>least</u> difficult

An adjective that ends in *y* usually forms the superlative degree by changing the *y* to *i* and adding -est.

handi<u>est</u>, clumsi<u>est</u>

Underline each adjective that is in the superlative degree.

1. That was the greatest movie I ever saw!

2. It had the most glamorous stars in the most exotic settings imaginable.

3. Even though the story was one of the tallest tales I've heard, I still enjoyed it.

4. The hero had to perform the most difficult stunts of all.

5. The special effects were the most intricate ever attempted.

6. The part of the heroine was played by the most talented actress in the world.

7. The villain was the nastiest character they could have found for the part.

8. The weakest part of the film was the ending.

9. It seems they selected the silliest conclusion possible.

Write four sentences of your own about a movie you have seen. Each sentence should include at least one adjective in the superlative degree. Underline the superlative degree adjectives.

10. _____

11. _____

12. _____

13. _____

Irregular Comparison of Adjectives

Some adjectives have an irregular form of comparison. An **irregular adjective** forms the degree of comparison by a complete change in the word itself.

Study the forms below before attempting the activity. Check a dictionary if you are in doubt about which form to use.

Positive	Comparative	Superlative
much	more	most
bad	worse	worst
good	better	best
far	farther	farthest
little	less	least

Underline the irregular form of each adjective.

1. That was the best meal he has ever cooked.

2. He won a prize at the reunion because he drove a farther distance than anyone else.

3. Hugo said he had a better day today than he had yesterday.

4. That is the worst poem I have ever read.

5. That is the most homework the class has ever been given.

6. The hungry girl ate less ham than eggs.

7. Of all the chefs, he added the least salt to his chili.

There are some adjectives that should not be compared because the positive degree is already the highest possible degree. For example, if something is empty, it cannot be emptier.

empty, correct, perfect, final, full, alone, wrong, supreme, single

Use the adjectives above to write sentences of your own.

8. _____

9. _____

10. _____

Limiting Adjectives

A **limiting adjective** is one that points out an object or indicates its number or quantity. The articles *a*, *an*, and *the* are limiting adjectives. *A* precedes a noun beginning with a consonant sound, and *an* precedes a noun beginning with a vowel sound.

the cat, a dog, an owl, an hour

Write **a** or **an** in front of each noun.

1. _____ garage   5. _____ DVD   9. _____ apple   13. _____ disaster

2. _____ ant   6. _____ baseball 10. _____ order   14. _____ concert

3. _____ honor   7. _____ sale   11. _____ elevator 15. _____ video

4. _____ car   8. _____ uncle   12. _____ carpet   16. _____ floor

A **numerical adjective** is a limiting adjective that indicates an exact number.

one, thirty, fifty

Circle the articles and underline the numerical adjectives.

17. The top speed limit on the interstate expressway is fifty-five miles per hour.

18. A two-hundred dollar fine may result if you speed.

19. There are only about five cars that pass this point every day.

20. Twenty police officers have been assigned to monitor the city streets.

21. If they save just one life, it will be worth the effort.

22. The traffic laws review book contained twenty-three pages.

23. I read the book ten times.

Write sentences about driving a car. Use a numerical adjective in each sentence.

24. _____

25. _____

26. _____

27. _____

28. _____

Demonstrative and Indefinite Adjectives

This, that, these, and *those* are **demonstrative adjectives** that point out a particular person, place, or thing. Use *this* and *these* for things close by and *that* and *those* for things distant in time or space.

Write a demonstrative adjective before each of the following objects.

1. _____ tulips (near)

2. _____ umbrella (far)

3. _____ boot (far)

4. _____ radio (far)

5. _____ tables (near)

6. _____ stadium (near)

7. _____ island (far)

8. _____ nation (far)

9. _____ empires (far)

10. _____ textbooks (near)

Circle the correct word or words.

11. (This, That) tree on the hill is beautiful.

12. (These, Those) musicians playing now are more talented than (these, those) musicians we heard last week.

13. (This, That) flower in my hand is more beautiful than the one in the vase.

14. (This, That) apple you are holding looks shinier than (this, that) one right there.

An **indefinite adjective** is an adjective that does not point out any one person, place or thing in particular.

<u>many</u> mice, <u>more</u> choices, <u>fewer</u> decisions

Circle the indefinite adjectives.

15. Some politicians seemed to be making many promises.

16. Few people could really understand what they wanted to do.

17. Several reporters tried to pin them down to the facts.

18. Many people in the crowd wanted an alternative.

19. Finally, more candidates came forward.

20. They talked like they understood many problems.

_____

Proper and Interrogative Adjectives

A **proper adjective** is an adjective formed from a proper noun. It is always capitalized and may contain more than one word.

Latin American dances, Florida oranges

1. Circle all of the adjectives and write **P** above each proper adjective.

Italian sauce	Mexican border	English language	purple book
new car	Greek salad	French bread	African stories
bright red apple	California sunshine	several shoes	English setter
Irish stew	Bastille Day parade	German dances	small puppy
million years	Chicago museum	Swedish meatballs	Michigan highway
Belgian waffles	Siamese cat	silk shirt	orange balloon
other classes	few animals	Japanese food	digital clock

An **interrogative adjective** is an adjective which is used to ask a question.

what, which

Circle each interrogative adjective and underline the noun it modifies.

2. Which part is missing from this computer?

3. What type of monitor do you have?

4. Which system works best for word processing?

5. What brand has the lowest price right now?

6. What store did you visit to look for a new computer?

Write a short paragraph about your neighborhood. Include two proper adjectives and two interrogative adjectives in the paragraph. Underline these adjectives.

_____

_____

_____

Predicate Adjectives

A **predicate adjective** follows a linking verb and describes the subject.
The fish was <u>fantastic</u>.

Underline each linking verb and circle each predicate adjective.

1. Bees are necessary for the process of pollination to be completed.

2. Honey from the hives is delicious.

3. The color is golden.

4. Worker bees are very industrious.

5. In the hierarchy of the hive, the queen bee is supreme.

6. The eggs are tiny.

7. Orchard owners are dependent on bees for their livelihood.

8. They are happy to see the swarms of bees invade their trees.

9. The mites which attack the hive are tiny.

10. They are unpopular with everyone.

11. Write a short paragraph using at least three predicate adjectives. Underline the predicate adjectives.

_____

_____

_____

_____

Use each linking verb to write a sentence that includes predicate adjectives.

12. are _____

13. were _____

14. is _____

15. was _____

Adverbs of Time

An **adverb** is a word that modifies a verb, an adjective, or another adverb. Adverbs indicate time, place, or manner.

Adverbs of time answer the question *when* or *how often*. They usually modify verbs.

People <u>seldom</u> like to be given orders.

Circle each adverb of time and underline the verb it modifies.

1. People have always needed some form of government.

2. First came dictatorships of one form or another.

3. Then, the king or dictator made all of the decisions.

4. Eventually, the ancient Greeks established a form of government they called democracy.

5. It was called democracy, but the people who did not own land could never vote.

6. Later, the Romans adapted this system into a republican form of government.

7. Under this system, the results were often representative of the people's wishes.

8. This form was always better than the totalitarian forms which eventually followed.

9. Totalitarian governments frequently allow human rights abuses.

10. Today, people everywhere look to the United States as a model of democracy.

11. They often feel that the democratic system works better than any other.

12. Even Americans are constantly working to improve their democratic system.

13. There is always room for improvement in any system.

Use the adverbs of time to write sentences about a historical event you have studied recently. Underline the verbs that are being modified.

14. finally _____

15. seldom _____

16. already _____

17. frequently _____

Adverbs of Place

Adverbs of place answer the question *where*. They usually modify verbs.

The fish swam <u>below</u>.

Circle each adverb of place and underline the verb it modifies.

1. People have looked everywhere for a satisfactory type of government.

2. The Japanese stayed away from the democratic style.

3. They preferred a government system which developed nearby.

4. Back in the mid-600s, an emperor ruled there.

5. Sailors came here from Europe in 1543.

6. Japan focused inward during the 1630s.

7. In 1854, Commodore Perry brought in US trade.

8. By 1868, the emperor looked outside for ideas to modernize Japan.

9. This technology spread out from the leaders to the people.

10. Today, many Western nations look there for ways to improve their own economies.

11. Write a short paragraph using three adverbs of place. Circle the adverbs of place and underline the verbs they modify.

_____

_____

_____

_____

Use the adverbs of place to write sentences. Underline the verbs that the adverbs modify.

12. underneath _____

13. away _____

14. inside _____

15. downward _____

Adverbs of Manner

Adverbs of manner answer the question *how* or in *what manner*. They usually end in *-ly*.
Do your work <u>thoroughly</u>.

Circle each adverb of manner and underline the verb it modifies.

1. People all over the world eagerly play association football, known in the United States as soccer.

2. Beginners must listen carefully to understand the rules.

3. When they understand completely, they will be ready to play the game.

4. The round ball must be carefully controlled.

5. Soccer can easily be played almost anywhere.

6. It is exciting to watch players gracefully execute complex foot movements.

7. Fans react emotionally when their favorite team loses.

8. The game was first played competitively in Great Britain in the late 1800s.

9. Games like soccer were played passionately by the Chinese in the third century BC.

10. The sport spread rapidly from Great Britain throughout the world.

11. The World Cup is the most avidly watched match in the world.

12. The World Cup is only played every four years.

13. Americans found out that it is a game that must be played intensely.

14. Athletes must be able to run quickly for long periods of time.

15. Fans in over 200 countries passionately cheer for their favorite team.

Write four sentences about a sport you like to play. Use an adverb of manner in each sentence. Circle the adverbs of manner and underline the verbs they modify.

16. _____

17. _____

18. _____

19. _____

Comparison of Adverbs

Like adjectives, many adverbs also have degrees of comparison. The three degrees of comparison are **positive**, **comparative**, and **superlative**. Some adverbs form the comparative degree by adding -*er* and the superlative degree by adding -*est*. Most adverbs that end in -*ly* form their comparative degrees by adding the word *more* or *less* in front of the positive degree. The superlative degree is formed by adding the word *most* or *least* in front of the positive degree.

1. Complete the chart with the missing adverbs   .

Positive	Comparative	Superlative
fast	faster	fastest
carefully	more/less carefully	most/least carefully
soon		
hard		
noisily		
late		
easily		
efficiently		
loudly		
proudly		
harshly		
neatly		
cheerfully		
courageously		
highly		

Circle each adverbs and indicate the degree of comparison: positive (**P**), comparative (**C**), or superlative (**S**).

_____ 2. In order to be a good goalie, you have to react more quickly than the average person.

_____ 3. The puck slides across the ice fast.

_____ 4. The teammate skating nearest will help you fend off the attack.

_____ 5. You might be pushed roughly onto the ice.

_____ 6. When a player has the puck, watch him or her more carefully.

Adverbs and Adjectives

> When trying to determine whether to use an adjective or an adverb, decide which word is being modified. Adjectives modify nouns and pronouns. Adverbs modify verbs, adjectives, and other adverbs.

Circle the correct word. Then, identify it by writing adverb (**ADV**) or adjective (**ADJ**) in the blank.

_____ 1. The soundtrack began very (strange, strangely).

_____ 2. There was a (sudden, suddenly) surge of volume.

_____ 3. Then an announcer (calm, calmly) listed the names of the cast.

_____ 4. It is not the (usual, usually) way for a film to begin.

_____ 5. The credits were (extreme, extremely) long.

_____ 6. (Gradual, Gradually) the actual movie started.

_____ 7. I had been (wise, wisely) to go out for popcorn during the credits.

_____ 8. But I felt (guilty, guiltily) because I didn't bring my sister any.

_____ 9. The plot moved (swift, swiftly) into a series of wild chases.

_____ 10. Each one was performed more (awkward, awkwardly) than the last.

_____ 11. The actors' performances were very (poor, poorly).

_____ 12. I can't remember when I saw a more (odd, oddly) movie.

_____ 13. I couldn't get out of there (quick, quickly) enough.

_____ 14. Next time, I'm going to read the review more (thorough, thoroughly).

Use the adjectives and adverbs in sentences. Circle the adjectives and adverbs and underline the words being modified.

15. clever _____

16. gradually _____

17. honest _____

18. genuinely _____

Interjections

Interjections are words that express strong feeling or sudden emotion. They may be followed by an exclamation point or a comma. Interjections are more effective when they are used sparingly.

Hey! Look at that hawk. Oh, that's a surprise.

Underline each interjection.

1. Wow! It's my birthday today!

2. Great! I can't wait for my friends to get here.

3. No! What do you mean they can't come?

4. Oh no! This is terrible!

5. Oh, quit complaining.

6. Rats! I thought this was going to be a great day.

7. Zounds! I have an idea!

8. Shh, listen.

9. Yes! This just might work.

10. Right! I'll call some of my other friends and see if they can come.

11. Ah, I love that idea.

12. Hey! Did you hear that?

13. Surprise! We came after all!

14. Gosh! I sure was worried for a while.

15. Super! It was a great celebration!

Use each interjection in a sentence.

16. hey _____

17. wow _____

18. alas _____

19. stop _____

Conjunctions

A **conjunction** is a word that joins words or groups of words together. Three types of conjunctions are **coordinating**, **correlative**, and **subordinating**.

Coordinating conjunctions: and, but, or, nor, for, yet, so

Correlative conjunctions: either—or, both—and, whether—or, neither—nor, not only—but also (These are always used in pairs.)

Some common **subordinating conjunctions**: after, although, as, as if, because, before, if, since, that, though, until, when, while

Circle each conjunction. Then, label each conjunction with coordinating (**CO**), correlative (**CR**), or subordinating (**SU**).

_____ 1. Moscow is Russia's largest city and its political capital as well.

_____ 2. It is also a commercial, cultural, and communications center.

_____ 3. It is known as a center for heavy machinery manufacturing, but it has other important industries.

_____ 4. Neither the czars nor the communist dictators were able to take the heart from Moscow's people.

_____ 5. We will understand the people of Moscow if we study their history.

_____ 6. Some of that history was hidden, though it is now coming to light.

_____ 7. Though Moscow remained an important center of culture and trade, St. Petersburg became the new capital.

_____ 8. Moscow was somewhat weakened because every effort was made to make St. Petersburg the center of attention.

_____ 9. This was encouraged for two centuries but was stopped in 1917 with the Russian Revolution.

_____ 10. The capital was once again Moscow when the government fell to the Bolsheviks.

_____ 11. Moscow grew rapidly in the 1930s and the city gained power.

_____ 12. During World War II, the German military not only used planes to bomb the city but also approached the city with foot soldiers.

Same Word—Different Part of Speech

There are many words whose function as a part of speech varies depending on how they are used in a particular sentence.

The answer was <u>right</u>. (adjective)

What <u>right</u> do you have to say that? (noun)

I will <u>right</u> all of the wrongs committed. (verb)

Identify the part of speech of each boldfaced word as an **adjective**, **adverb**, **noun**, **pronoun**, **verb**, or **preposition**.

_____ 1. He slid **down** head first.

_____ 2. Did you notice an unusual **smell** when you walked in?

_____ 3. **Some** are planning to visit the art museum while others are intending to go out for lunch.

_____ 4. The people of this **country** want real leadership.

_____ 5. The itsy-bitsy spider slid **down** the waterspout.

_____ 6. I **smell** a rat!

_____ 7. Delaina signed up for a class in **country** painting.

_____ 8. **Some** people really enjoyed the dance we went to last night.

_____ 9. Terrance said that it was the most moving **play** she had ever seen.

_____ 10. Hannah **played** with her little sister while I cooked dinner.

Write sentences using the words as the specified parts of speech.

11. musical (noun) _____

12. safe (adjective) _____

13. work (verb) _____

14. train (noun) _____

15. musical (adjective) _____

Identifying Parts of Speech—Review

Noun: names a person, place, thing, or idea

Pronoun: takes the place of a noun

Verb: shows action or state of being

Adjective: modifies a noun or pronoun

Adverb: modifies a verb, an adjective, or another adverb

Preposition: shows relationship of one noun or pronoun to another word

Conjunction: links words or groups of words

Interjection: expresses strong emotion or surprise

Identify the part of speech of the underlined word.

_____ 1. A city must be planned <u>carefully</u>, or people will not want to live in it.

_____ 2. We were going to attend the game, but the meteorologist <u>predicted</u> rain.

_____ 3. I am going to do <u>my</u> homework after school, but I would rather play with my friends.

_____ 4. Shauna put a <u>dollar</u> into the vending machine, but nothing came out.

_____ 5. Dawn skidded <u>around</u> the corner, and she lost control of the car.

_____ 6. The paperboy drove <u>past</u>, and he threw the paper into the bushes.

_____ 7. Wash the car <u>and</u> wax it.

_____ 8. My mother and I went to two movies and liked <u>both</u> of them.

_____ 9. How will you <u>pay</u> for this damage, and when can I expect the money?

_____ 10. Gerardo will examine the car, <u>though</u> Tristan will buy it.

_____ 11. The team won the game, and the <u>excited</u> crowd waited outside the stadium to cheer them.

_____ 12. <u>Wow</u>! Trent is going to visit the new museum.

Appositives

An **appositive** is a noun or noun phrase that further explains a noun. The appositive is usually next to the noun it is identifying or clarifying.

Mr. Lange, <u>our English teacher</u>, is very intelligent.

Underline the appositive and circle the noun it explains.

1. Kami, my older sister, left immediately.

2. His car, a vintage roadster, crashed.

3. That man, the village chief, will command.

4. Baseball, my favorite sport, ended yesterday.

5. The senator, a Democrat, voted today.

6. Mr. Tobias, our Latin teacher, was nominated and defeated.

7. His house, a rambling shack, burned down.

8. The dog, a huge German shepherd, jumped up.

9. The boat, a sleek cruiser, slid past.

10. My cat, a grey manx, stretched and yawned.

11. Did you see the film at Studio 28, the movie theater?

12. My favorite ice cream, butter pecan, was on sale.

Write sentences about four people you admire. Include an appositive in each sentence.

13. _____

14. _____

15. _____

16. _____

Pronouns: Who/Whom

The use of the pronouns *who* and *whom* is determined by the pronoun's function in the clause. Generally, *who* is used as a subject of a sentence or clause.

Who baked the cake?

The boy who baked it lives next door to me.

Whom is used as a direct object or an object of a preposition.

Whom did you visit last week?

With whom did you travel?

Circle the correct pronoun in each sentence.

1. Mr. Hagen is the one (who, whom) handles disciplinary matters.

2. Do you think he is one in (who, whom) you can put your trust?

3. Matthew is well acquainted with people (who, whom) will tell the truth.

4. She is the person with (who, whom) you should speak.

5. (Who, Whom) is waiting for me?

6. For (who, whom) do you think we should vote?

7. To (who, whom) do you wish to speak?

8. The girl (who, whom) we met is very intelligent.

9. Penny, (who, whom) is my youngest sister, is going to become a doctor.

10. The person to (who, whom) you spoke is no longer here.

11. (Who, Whom) went to the play?

12. With (who, whom) did you see the movie?

13. My brother, (who, whom) lives in Georgia, likes to jog.

14. (Who, Whom) is coming to the party?

Using the pronouns *who* and *whom*, write a short paragraph on another sheet of paper about something that you have studied in another class.

Punctuating Direct Quotations

Quotation marks are used to enclose direct quotations. The end punctuation usually comes before the final quotation mark at the end of the quote.

Mary said, "Where are we going?"

Always capitalize the first word of a direct quotation. Do not capitalize the first word in the second part of an interrupted quote unless the second part begins a new sentence.

"When it starts to snow," he said, "put on your heavy coat."

"Where did he go?" Bob asked. "We need him."

Punctuate and add capitals to the sentences.

1. look out jackie cried

_____

2. didn't you see that broken step Jackie asked

_____

3. no Ahmad said thanks for warning me

_____

4. i think we should fix that before someone gets hurt Jackie suggested

_____

5. do you know where there's a hammer Ahmad queried

_____

6. i don't Jackie admitted but maybe Emily does

_____

7. hey Emily she yelled where's the hammer

_____

8. don't yell Emily responded i'm right behind you

_____

Write three sentences with direct quotations on another sheet of paper. Include at least one interrogative and one exclamatory quotation.

Direct/Indirect Quotations

A **direct quotation** is the use of someone's exact words. It is always set off with quotation marks.

> Kati said, "I am going to the beach today."

An **indirect quotation** is the writer's description of someone else's words. It does not require quotation marks.

> Dave said that Kati was going to the beach today.

Write direct quotation (**DQ**) or indirect quotation (**IQ**). Then, add quotation marks wherever they are needed.

_____ 1. Pilar said, We're going to the Winter Olympics!

_____ 2. How are you getting there? Jaime asked.

_____ 3. At the same time, Demetri asked Phoebe what her favorite event was.

_____ 4. We're flying, Pilar said, and I can't wait to go!

_____ 5. Jose said that he'd never flown in an airplane.

_____ 6. Pilar then said her faviorite event is figure skating.

_____ 7. Are you really going to see the figure skating? Ashton asked.

_____ 8. Pilar said, Yes, my father has already bought tickets.

_____ 9. Well, I'd rather see the downhill skiing, Jaime interjected.

_____ 10. Ashton said that she would rather not worry about people getting hurt.

_____ 11. Demetri said that he understood what Anne was talking about.

_____ 12. May I come along with you? Demetri implored.

Write two sentences that contain direct quotations and two sentences that contain indirect quotations.

13. (direct) _____

14. (direct) _____

15. (indirect) _____

16. (indirect) _____

Other Uses for Quotation Marks

Single quotation marks are used to set off a quotation within a quotation.

"When did you tell me, 'I'm going with you'?" Dad asked.

The commercial asked, "How do you spell *relief*?"

Quotation marks are used to set off words, phrases, or sentences referred to within a sentence.

You spell *relief* "r-e-l-i-e-f."

Quotation marks are used to set off slang words and expressions.

The pitcher threw the batter a "spitter."

Quotation marks are used to set off the titles of magazine articles, names of songs, titles of poems, and chapters of books.

The top story in the magazine was entitled "Dog Tales."

Add quotation marks where needed.

1. Chicago is my favorite poem, Bill said.

2. That's just because you grew up there, Rick replied.

3. That's not true, Bill corrected. I like the way Sandburg writes.

4. When Bill said, I like the way Sandburg writes, I think he really meant it, added Hestor.

5. Did you do your homework yet? Benji asked.

6. I read the chapter Tropical Rainforests in my science book, added Hestor·

7. Ingrid started singing Auld Lang Syne.

8. The class read The Seven Ages of Man.

9. Sabena wondered if Rules of the Game was included in the book of short stories.

10. The term short story is defined in the glossary.

11. Norman wondered what authors the teacher considered flaky.

12. What kind of question is that? asked the teacher.

13. Is that word in the dictionary? Alexa inquired.

14. Did Norman say, I'll look that up? inquired the teacher.

Inverted Sentence Order

Sometimes part or all of the verb comes before the subject in a sentence. Sentences in which this happens are called **inverted sentences**. *Inverted* means that the order is reversed.

Is Bill finished with the dictionary?

On the corner is the best ice-cream store in town.

Have you heard the new song?

If you had trouble finding the subject and predicate in any of the above sentences, try rearranging the subject and predicate.

Bill is finished with the dictionary.

The best ice-cream store in town is on the corner.

You have heard the new song.

Draw one line under the simple subject and two lines under the verb.

1. What is the capital of Australia?

2. Isn't it Canberra?

3. In the hills near Canberra is the prettiest scenery in Australia.

4. Nearby are the homes of koalas and wombats.

5. There is the home of the kookaburra, also.

6. Here is a map of Australia.

7. Will you ever go to Australia?

8. Have you been there?

9. Aren't there rain forests on the Queensland coast?

10. Off the Queensland coast is the Great Barrier Reef.

11. Is Australia a country as well as a continent?

12. With whom does Australia trade?

Subject Complements

A **subject complement** is a word that comes after a linking verb and refers back to the subject. Subject complements can be nouns, pronouns, or adjectives.

A noun used as a subject complement is called a **predicate noun**.

> The ruby is a <u>gem</u>.

A pronoun used as a subject complement is called a **predicate pronoun**.

> The ruby is <u>it</u>.

An adjective used as a subject complement is called a **predicate adjective**.

> The ruby is <u>red</u>.

Underline each simple subject. Then, circle the subject complement. Label each with **(PN)** for predicate noun, **(PPN)** for predicate pronoun, or **(PA)** for predicate adjective.

_____ 1.   A person who studies minerals is a mineralogist.

_____ 2.   Minerals are useful.

_____ 3.   Minerals that make metals are ore minerals.

_____ 4.   All minerals are uniquely beautiful.

_____ 5.   Emeralds are green.

_____ 6.   One very strong mineral is the diamond.

_____ 7.   If you're looking for a very hard mineral, the diamond is it.

_____ 8.   No mineral is harder.

_____ 9.   Graphite, however, is very soft.

_____ 10.   The black substance in a pencil that leaves a mark on paper is it.

_____ 11.   One property of minerals is specific gravity.

_____ 12.   Having a very high specific gravity, gold ore is extremely heavy.

_____ 13.   The hobby of mineral collecting is popular.

_____ 14.   Occasionally, obtaining certain minerals is a challenge.

_____ 15.   Minerals are the most common solid materials on Earth.

Direct Objects

A **direct object** is a noun or pronoun that follows an action verb. It tells *who* or *what* receives the action of the verb.

The flood washed out <u>the road</u>.

To find the direct object, ask *who* or *what* after the action verb.

Question: The flood washed out what?

Answer: the road (direct object)

Circle each action verb and underline each direct object.

1. The Polar Bears won the championship.

2. Daysha answered the question.

3. Without delay, Jasper boarded the train.

4. The salesclerk in the department store sold every pink shirt in stock.

5. The leader sent the troops into the battle.

6. The student read the newspaper every day.

7. The three networks immediately sent reporters to the crime scene.

8. Macon gave a check to the charitable organization.

9. The principal grabbed the basketball.

10. Father wants us to return the car as soon as possible.

11. The French teacher sponsors the Honor Society.

12. The enthusiastic boy joined the team.

13. Nina won the prize at the fair last summer.

14. The clown wearing the polka-dotted hat threw the balloon.

Write two sentences and include a noun used as a direct object in each. Underline the direct objects and circle the action verbs.

15. _____

16. _____

Indirect Objects

An **indirect object** is a noun or pronoun that names the person *to whom* or *for whom* something is done.

   Mario served <u>the guests</u> raw fish.

To find the indirect object, ask *to whom* or *for whom* after the action verb.

   Question: Mario served raw fish to whom?

   Answer: <u>the guests</u> (indirect object)

Underline each indirect object and circle each action verb.

1. Paul told him the bad news.

2. The director taught the choir a new song.

3. Gabriel gave Shannon a symbol of his love.

4. I sent Bailey a postcard from France.

5. The farmer fed the geese the corn.

6. The star goalie left me two tickets at the gate.

7. The boss handed his employee the broom.

8. The book won her instant fame.

9. The window in the office offered the clients a good view.

10. Maria offered the secretary a piece of cake.

11. Simone gave them her trophy to put in the display case.

Write three sentences and include an indirect object in each. Underline the indirect objects once, the direct objects twice, and circle the action verbs.

12. _____

13. _____

14. _____

Objects of Prepositions

A noun or pronoun used as the **object of a preposition** follows the preposition, though there may be modifiers of the noun that come between it and the preposition.

> She waited in <u>the building</u>.
>
> Quan gave the book to <u>him</u>.

To find the object, ask *whom* or *what* after the preposition.

> She waited in what?   the building
>
> Quan gave the book to whom?   him

Underline each entire prepositional phrase and circle the object of the preposition.

1.   We all hoped to see Tyesha on Thanksgiving Day.

2.   She was driving to see us from her home two hours away.

3.   Sara scurried into her bedroom.

4.   I told her it was time for Tyesha to arrive in the car.

5.   Her response was to crawl farther under her bed.

6.   Sara wanted to grab Tyesha's ankle when she walked by the bed.

7.   Then, we heard someone in the kitchen.

8.   Just to be safe, I looked in the phone book and dialed the police.

9.   Tyesha found a turkey sandwich in the refrigerator.

10. We did not know she had arrived at our house early.

11. She was surprised when the police pulled into the driveway.

Write three sentences about a holiday. Each sentence should include a prepositional phrase. Underline the entire prepositional phrase and circle the object of the preposition.

12. _____

13. _____

14. _____

Adjective Prepositional Phrases

A **prepositional phrase** is a group of words that shows how two nouns or pronouns are related to each other. It can function as an adjective or an adverb depending on the word it modifies. Like a one-word adjective, an adjective prepositional phrase modifies a noun or pronoun.

The shady ground <u>under the elm tree</u> was perfect.

Underline each prepositional phrase and circle the words being modified.

1. People in the news are frequently embarrassed.

2. The drugstore in town is open today.

3. The musical with the best choreography will win.

4. A gorilla in a red jumpsuit and a chimpanzee in a chiffon dress ran into the tent.

5. The cottage beside the gurgling brook was sold a year ago.

6. The list of students' addresses was burned in the fire this morning.

7. Nobody in this class knows.

8. The doctors in this hospital are working very hard.

9. The combination to the safe is lost.

10. The graphics on the computer are amazing.

Write sentences using the prepositional phrases as adjectives. Underline the prepositional phrases and circle the prepositions.

11. for the defense _____

12. beside the lake _____

13. below the green umbrella _____

14. above the slimy seaweed _____

15. amid the thick fog _____

16. with the red flag _____

17. on the sailboat _____

Adverb Prepositional Phrases

Like a one-word adverb, an **adverb prepositional phrase** usually modifies a verb and may tell where, how, or when an action takes place.

We play ball <u>in the park</u>. (tells where we play)

She called <u>in a loud voice</u>. (tells how she called)

Mom gave us smiles <u>throughout the day</u>. (tells when Mom gave)

Underline each prepositional phrase and circle the words being modified.

1. The stands sagged under the students' weight.

2. My biology book fell into the puddle.

3. Roxanne, the champion runner, jumped over the hurdle with ease.

4. The gifts were wrapped with care and placed under the tree.

5. Mason and Tiffany walked under the bridge.

6. Several jumpers pushed from the plane too early.

7. The firefighters rushed into the forest.

8. After the defeat, the team traveled alone through the night.

9. You will find Gerardo sitting behind the barn.

10. The Amish travel everywhere in their buggies.

11. The birds flew into the tree.

12. The girl danced with graceful movements.

13. Lightning flashes around the clouds.

14. A tornado moves with shocking speed.

Write sentences using the prepositional phrases as adverbs. Underline the prepositional phrases and circle the prepositions.

15. in another language _____

16. in his math class _____

17. under the bed _____

Recognizing Sentences

A **sentence** expresses a complete thought. It should begin with a capital letter and end with a period (**.**), a question mark(**?**), or an exclamation point (**!**).

For each complete sentence, write **OK** next to it. If a group of words is not a sentence, add words to make it a sentence and write the sentence on the line.

_____ 1. Portugal is in Europe.

_____

_____ 2. On the same peninsula as Spain.

_____

_____ 3. Both countries occupy the Iberian Peninsula.

_____

_____ 4. Bordered by the Mediterranean Sea and the Atlantic Ocean.

_____

_____ 5. Portugal is much smaller than Spain.

_____

_____ 6. It has a different language, although Portuguese is similar to Spanish.

_____

_____ 7. Because both languages are based on Latin.

_____

_____ 8. Why do you want to go to Portugal?

_____

_____ 9. To see the beautiful scenery, which is world famous.

_____

_____ 10. Visiting Portugal has always been my dream.

_____

Sentences and Fragments

> A **sentence** is a group of words which expresses a complete thought.
>> We went to the party.
>>
>> Will you go to the party with me?
>
> A **fragment** is a group of words punctuated like a sentence but not expressing a complete thought.
>> When we left the party.
>>
>> And then the cake.

Label each group of words with (**S**) sentence or (**F**) fragment.

_____ 1. You should go to the doctor for a physical.

_____ 2. A visit to the dentist makes me nervous.

_____ 3. Shots in the arm.

_____ 4. People in the waiting room.

_____ 5. Always tell the doctor exactly where it hurts.

_____ 6. When the nurse comes in.

_____ 7. Did you have any cavities this time?

_____ 8. The surgery was successful.

_____ 9. If you go to the hospital.

_____ 10. He filled out the medical form incorrectly.

_____ 11. Then the doctor.

_____ 12. Are you feeling better now?

_____ 13. I feel wonderful!

_____ 14. Please make me some more soup.

Add words before or after the fragments to construct complete sentences.

15. When I broke my arm. _____

16. If you go to visit Henry. _____

Fragments

A sentence contains a subject and a verb and expresses a complete thought. A group of words that is punctuated like a sentence but does not contain a complete thought is called a **fragment**. Often, the reason the fragment does not express a complete thougnt is that it lacks a subject or verb.

Went home past the supermarket.

The reason I missed school yesterday.

Sometimes you can correct a fragment by adding a word or words. Other times, you can make the correction by connecting the fragment to a sentence and changing the punctuation.

Incorrect: On the way to school, I saw Amy. And her brother.

Correct: On the way to school, I saw Amy and her brother.

Correct each fragment by adding a word or words to make a complete sentence. Change capital letters and punctuation where necessary.

1. who is the best player on the team.

   _____

2. Opened the package and put it carefully on the table.

   _____

3. Jumped straight up and scored the basket.

   _____

Correct each fragment by connecting it to the accompanying sentence. Change capital letters and punctuation where necessary.

4. Many people don't like abstract art. Because they don't understand it.

   _____

5. The abstract movement was started by gifted artists. Such as Miró and Kandinsky.

   _____

6. They thought art was becoming too realistic. Looking just like photography.

   _____

Run-ons

A **run-on** is two or more complete sentences written without proper punctuation between them.

Run-ons: Ballet is exhausting work, you have to be in great shape to be a dancer.

It looks easy it's really hard. It's beautiful ballet is my favorite activity.

Run-ons can be corrected in three ways.

1. If the two sentences are closely related, they can be separated by a semicolon.
   Correct: Ballet is exhausting work; you have to be in great shape to be a dancer.

2. Closely related sentences can also be separated with a comma and a conjunction.
   Correct: It looks easy, but it's really hard.

3. Sentences that are not as closely related can be separated with a period.
   Correct: It's beautiful. Ballet is my favorite activity.

Correct each run-on by rewriting the sentences correctly.

_____ 1. Studying leaves is fascinating there are so many different kinds.

_____

_____ 2. Leaves come in different shades of green no two kinds seem to be the same.

_____

_____ 3. Leaves that grow in low light are usually dark green leaves that grow in bright light are lighter green.

_____

_____ 4. A leaf's shape is important experts can tell a lot about a tree from the shape of its leaves.

_____

_____ 5. Leaves from rain forest plants often have drip tips these are pointed tips that help water run off the leaf.

_____

_____ 6. Some leaves have complicated shapes these shapes allow the wind to blow the leaf without tearing it.

_____

Run-On Sentences: Review

Correct the run-ons by adding the proper punctuation and conjunctions if necessary. If a sentence is not a run-on, write **OK** on the line.

_____ 1. The moray eel conceals himself by hiding in the rocks he pops his head out to catch his prey.

_____ 2. A group of sea animals shoots water through one of two body openings they are named sea squirts.

_____ 3. Starfish and sea urchins have no heads they have mouths on their bellies.

_____ 4. Starfish have five flexible arms they use them to walk around.

_____ 5. A seahorse is a fish that swims in an upright position the male has a kangaroo-like pouch that holds the fertilized eggs until they hatch.

_____ 6. Most sea urchins are vegetarians or scavengers most are equipped with five sharp teeth for scraping food.

_____ 7. Sand dollars are shallow-water echnioderms their bodies are covered with spines that aid in locomotion.

_____ 8. Seaweed is commonly found along rocky beaches it grows attached to the rocks.

_____ 9. Female sea turtles come ashore to lay their eggs in holes they dig the holes and then cover them with sand.

_____ 10. A sea otter's hind feet are broadened into flippers his forefeet are useful for grasping.

_____ 11. The sea cucumber is a type of sea animal with a long, fleshy body it belongs to the echinoderm group.

_____ 12. Gulls are long-winged birds they are often seen flying and dipping over large bodies of water.

_____ 13. Scientists still don't even know all the basic facts about famous sea life the habits of great white sharks have been puzzling them for years.

_____ 14. Many people are afraid of sharks some people are not.

_____ 15. Aquariums are places that try to teach people about fish and marine life an aquarium's tanks are very difficult to maintain.

_____ 16. Educating people about sea life is the job of a marine biologist this is a highly specialized field of study.

Simple Subjects and Predicates

The **simple subject** names the person or thing the sentence is about. It does not include articles or modifying words.

   The girl in the red hat ran to the corner.

The **simple predicate** tells what the subject is or does. It does not include any modifying words. The simple predicate is a verb or a verb phrase.

   The main city library is expanding its shelves.

   John Maynard Keynes was an economist.

Underline the simple subject once and the simple predicate twice.

1.   One African bird is named the honey guide.

2.   The favorite food of the honey guide is beeswax from the nests of wild bees.

3.   The nests are too strong for the honey guide, though.

4.   So the clever bird enlists the aid of an ally.

5.   The unlikely ally is an animal called the ratel.

6.   The black and white ratel is called the "honey badger" by many people.

7.   Rich, sweet honey is the ratel's favorite food.

8.   The ratel's thick, loose skin resists bee stings.

9.   The smart bird finds a bees' nest.

10. It chatters to the ratel.

11. The chattering bird leads the ratel to the nest.

12. The ratel breaks the nest with its strong claws.

13. The hungry animal eats the honey.

14. Then the happy bird eats the wax from the broken nest.

Complete Subjects and Predicates

The **complete subject** of a sentence tells what the sentence is about. It may be one word or many words.

The boy from Barcelona is the world geography champion.

He knew the answer to every question they asked him.

The **complete predicate** tells what the subject is or does. It may be one word or many.

He knew the answer to every question they asked him.

The young student won.

Underline the complete subject once and the complete predicate twice.

1. The people in many parts of the world are unable to feed themselves in times of disaster.

2. International relief agencies and many governments send aid to those people.

3. The most famous international relief agency is the Red Cross.

4. The Red Cross was founded in 1864 to aid victims of war.

5. Red Cross workers fight misery in times of both war and peace.

6. Over 135 nations have Red Cross societies.

7. Each Red Cross society runs its own program.

8. The American Red Cross has more than 10 million volunteers.

9. Voluntary contributions fund the programs and services of the American Red Cross.

10. All aid to disaster victims is free.

11. Write a short paragraph about an organization whose purpose you admire. Underline the complete subjects once and complete predicates twice.

_____

_____

_____

_____

_____

Compound Subjects and Predicates

A **compound subject** contains two or more subjects usually joined by *and* or *or*.

Mark Twain and Harper Lee are American authors.

A **compound predicate** has two or more predicates usually joined by *and, or,* or *but*.

They wrote great novels and became famous.

Turn each subject into a compound subject and write the new sentence on the line. If necessary, change the verb to agree with the compound subject.

1. Quincy is the best student in math class.

    _____

2. Sycamore trees are my favorite trees.

    _____

3. Birds live in trees.

    _____

4. Light is necessary for a plant to grow.

    _____

Turn each predicate into a compound predicate using *and, or,* or *but*. Write each new sentence on the line.

5. Mackenzie dribbled to the foul line.

    _____

6. Evan painted a picture for the show.

    _____

7. My father lit the barbecue.

    _____

8. Noah bought a new DVD.

    _____

Agreement of Subject and Verb

A verb must agree with its subject in number. That is, a singular subject requires a singular verb, and a plural subject requires a plural verb.

    Singular: The <u>tree</u> <u>sways</u> in the wind.

    Plural: The <u>trees</u> <u>sway</u> in the wind.

The number of the subject is not changed by a phrase or clause that might follow it.

    The <u>tree</u> with dozens of coconuts <u>sways</u> in the wind.

    The <u>trees</u> on this island <u>sway</u> in the wind.

Circle each correct verb choice.

1. A single lightning bolt (is, are) capable of doing a great deal of damage.

2. The peak temperature of a bolt (heats, heat) the surrounding air to over 60,000°F (33,315°C).

3. The lightning stroke (create, creates) a jagged picture across the sky.

4. Commercial jets (is, are) seldom hit by lightning.

5. If struck, they (suffer, suffers) only slight damage.

6. Planes (has, have) special shielding to protect their electronic equipment.

7. Rocket launches (provide, provides) the best chance to study lightning.

8. Photography (is, are) another way to study lightning.

9. Scientists in many labs (think, thinks) that there is even lightning on Venus.

10. A bolt of lightning from the clouds (is, are) always an awesome sight.

11. Write a short paragraph describing what it would be like to be caught out in a boat during a storm. Underline each verb and circle each subject.

_____

_____

_____

_____

_____

Subject and Object Pronouns

When a pronoun is the subject of the sentence, it is called a **subject pronoun**.

He caught the ball. (subject)

When a pronoun is used as the direct object, indirect object, or object of a preposition, it is called an **object pronoun**.

Sally saw us. (direct object)

Matthew throws us the balls. (indirect object)

Todd threw the ball to us. (object of preposition)

Circle each pronoun used as a subject. Underline each pronoun used as an object.

1. We will never allow it to happen in this school.

2. After thinking about it carefully, he decided to go anyway.

3. Even though the fruit was spoiled, the grocer sold it at the same price.

4. They told us that this was going to be a very exciting day.

5. I decided how the money should be spent.

6. I wanted her to help me make the decision.

7. She refused to do this.

8. Harry wanted to buy it at the fruit stand.

9. They did not stock apricot jam there.

10. He told them about a grocery store located several blocks away.

11. Olivia told me about a movie.

12. We chatted about it while walking to the store.

13. Write a short paragraph about a real or imagined visit to another country using at least three subject pronouns and three object pronouns.

_____

_____

_____

_____

Independent and Dependent Clauses

An **independent clause** is a group of words with a subject and a predicate that expresses a complete thought and can stand by itself as a sentence.

Jack played golf until it was too dark to see.

A **dependent clause** cannot stand alone. It depends upon the independent clause of the sentence to complete its meaning. Dependent clauses start with words like *who, which, that, because, when, if, until, before,* and *after.*

If the people support Hank, he will run.

Underline each independent clause once and each dependent clause twice.

1. When the cold weather arrives, I'm going south.

2. The class really enjoyed the movie that showed life under the sea.

3. If you think you know the answer, raise your hand.

4. I was about to leave for my vacation when I noticed that the tire was flat.

5. Felipe really liked the car that we bought for him at the auction.

6. Trisha was really disappointed that we could not go.

7. Until history became Henry's favorite subject, it was not easy for him.

8. When David builds a new radio-controlled car, we're going to race each other.

9. The cottage that we had purchased was old and dilapidated.

10. If the pain does not go away, please call the doctor.

11. Sheila knows many people who can play bridge.

12. Tia thought she knew just how he felt because she'd had the same experience.

13. I have not yet heard the song that the popular singer recorded in Finnish.

14. The paramedics grabbed the oxygen when they saw the patient turning blue.

15. You have not lived until you take a trip down the Colorado River in a raft.

16. When I returned to the store, he had already left.

Adjective Clauses

An **adjective clause** is a dependent clause that functions as an adjective. It can modify any noun or pronoun in a sentence.

The politician <u>who won the election</u> saluted his supporters.

Underline each adjective clause and circle the word it modifies.

1. Shane knows the teacher who gave you the detention.

2. Traditions that seem to have disappeared often return.

3. The painter tried to match the color that was used before.

4. The activity that Iesha most enjoyed was diving from the falls.

5. I bought the desk that was in the front window.

6. He put his hand under the table that had been freshly painted.

7. Sally is the person who applied for the job.

8. The police officer whose gun fell from his holster was very embarrassed.

9. The lake where they caught all of the fish was far away.

10. The city that we visited was one of the cleanest in the area.

11. The play to which the critic referred was a failure.

12. The horse that I liked fell during the race.

13. You will have to tell me the names of the students who might help us.

14. A wall that faces south will absorb a lot of solar heat.

Write four sentences about your neighborhood. Include an adjective clause in each. Underline each adjective clause and circle the noun or pronoun it modifies.

15. _____

16. _____

17. _____

18. _____

Adjective Clauses

An **adjective clause** is a dependent clause that functions as an adjective. It can modify any noun or pronoun in a sentence. Adjective clauses tell which one, what kind, or how many.

Some of the animals <u>that live in the wild</u> have claws.

Underline each adjective clause and circle the word it modifies.

1. Feline claws, which are used to catch prey, are retractable.

2. An owl's claws, which are called talons, are dangerous weapons.

3. Rather than claws, orangutans possess fingers that have fingerprints much like a human's.

4. A polar bear uses his front paws and short, sharp claws for holding on to prey that is slippery.

5. There are five fingers on a panda's hand and five toes on each foot, which all have long, sharp claws.

6. Playful lion cubs, who must learn to hunt, use their claws to snag anything that moves.

7. The hoof of a giraffe, which has no claws, makes a print larger than a dinner plate.

8. The fishing bat, which hunts fish swimming near the water's surface, swoops down and uses its long claws to grab the fish.

9. With her back legs, the female turtle digs a hole that she will use to protect her eggs.

10. A parrot has two toes that point forward and two toes that point backward.

11. Wolf babies are born underground in dens that are often dug by the wolves' parents.

12. Claws that are found on the feet of birds, reptiles, and mammals are often sharp, hooked structures.

13. A dog's toenails, which grow long, need to be cut regularly.

14. All claws, nails, talons, horns, and hooves are made of the same material, which is hardened cells of the epidermis, the outer layer of skin.

Adverb Clauses

An **adverb clause** is a dependent clause that functions as an adverb. It can modify a verb, an adjective, or another adverb. Adverb clauses tell how, when, where, or why an action happened.

　　We ate <u>when Grandpa arrived</u>. (modifies *ate*; tells when)

Underline each adverb clause and write the question it answers: **how, when, where,** or **why**.

_____ 1. You should listen carefully when the teacher speaks.

_____ 2. Because I read the book, I disliked the movie.

_____ 3. The doctor was very nervous before he began the surgery.

_____ 4. Everything began when Jay entered the room.

_____ 5. Ellen's reading will be the last because it is the best.

_____ 6. Because you have been so nice, I will allow you to move ahead of me.

_____ 7. Before Jessi started running, she felt tired all the time.

_____ 8. He looked where the backpack was last seen.

_____ 9. I can stay afloat by moving my arms.

_____ 10. After the class is over, I will tell you a secret about the professor.

_____ 11. When you get to the light, turn left.

_____ 12. She practiced every day because she wanted to join the team.

_____ 13. Since the book was about dogs, I found it interesting.

Write four sentences about a hobby you enjoy. For each sentence, include an adverb clause which answers the indicated question.

14. (how) _____

15. (when) _____

16. (where) _____

17. (why) _____

Noun Clauses

A **noun clause** is a dependent clause that functions as a noun. It may be used as a subject, a direct object, an indirect object, an object of a preposition, or a predicate noun.

Subject: <u>What happened</u> surprised everyone.

Direct object: George wondered <u>what he could do</u>.

Indirect object: Alyson will give <u>whoever wants one</u> a cookie.

Object of preposition: The children did not laugh until <u>the end of the play</u>.

Predicate noun: The problem is <u>what we will eat when we get there</u>.

Underline each noun clause and indicate how the clause is used in the sentence by writing **(S)** subject, **(DO)** direct object, **(IO)** indirect object, **(OP)** object of a preposition, or **(PN)** predicate noun.

_____ 1.   That you should eat your vegetables is certainly true.

_____ 2.   What Heather did today was very difficult.

_____ 3.   The meteorologists agreed that rain was expected.

_____ 4.   The bus will depart at whatever time you designate.

_____ 5.   A good movie is what I would like to see today.

_____ 6.   I will give whomever comes to the door the message.

_____ 7.   Whose books these are is obvious.

_____ 8.   This prize will be awarded to whoever completes the course.

_____ 9.   Life is what you make it.

_____ 10. What you say is not the truth.

_____ 11. How a computer works is a mystery to me.

_____ 12. Whoever wrote this graffiti will be punished.

_____ 13. A chance at the big time was what the minor league players craved.

_____ 14. I know that this plan will work.

Write five sentences on another sheet of paper. For each sentence, include a noun clause used as a direct object, a subject, a predicate noun, an object of a preposition, or an indirect object. Underline the noun clause and indicate how the clause is used in the sentence.

Noun Clauses

A **noun clause** may be used as a subject, a direct object, an indirect object, an object of a preposition, or a predicate noun.

Subject: <u>What occurred</u> was not planned at all.

Direct object: They wondered <u>what they should do</u> now.

Indirect object: Should they make <u>whoever broke the window</u> pay the bill?

Object of the preposition: I was grateful to <u>whoever would clean up the mess</u>.

Predicate noun: The good thing was <u>that no one was hurt</u>.

Underline each noun clause and indicate how the clause is used in the sentence by writing **(S)** subject, **(DO)** direct object, **(IO)** indirect object, **(OP)** object of a preposition, or **(PN)** predicate noun.

_____ 1. Felicia and Derrick considered what they could do to earn money.

_____ 2. Felicia thought that her idea might work.

_____ 3. What Felicia proposed was to start their own window-washing business.

_____ 4. That people would want their windows cleaned seemed obvious to Derrick.

_____ 5. How to get the proper equipment was what they had to figure out first.

_____ 6. Then, whatever they could promise to persuade their customers they printed in their advertisement fliers.

_____ 7. They would give whoever called in the first week a discount price.

_____ 8. Felicia and Derrick agreed that the fliers should be hand-delivered.

_____ 9. Their initial week of washing windows was pretty much what they expected.

_____ 10. Whoever had the dirtiest windows seemed to call for service.

_____ 11. That you should keep your word was their business motto.

_____ 12. So, Felicia and Derrick gave whomever called a 50 percent discount that first week.

_____ 13. Throughout the summer, they worked hard for whomever they could.

Identifying Clauses

An **adjective clause** is a dependent clause that functions as an adjective modifying nouns or pronouns.

An **adverb clause** is a dependent clause that functions as an adverb modifying verbs, adjectives, or other adverbs.

A **noun clause** is a dependent clause that functions as a noun.

Underline each dependent clause and indicate if it is an adjective clause (**ADJ**), an adverb clause (**ADV**), or a noun clause (**N**).

_____ 1. Dave read the pamphlet to whoever would listen.

_____ 2. How you play the game is important.

_____ 3. Green is a color that is considered soothing.

_____ 4. I would like you to wait so that we can go together.

_____ 5. We already know what his real problem is.

_____ 6. The tornado that hit the town destroyed many homes.

_____ 7. Greg eats hot dogs when he is at the ball park.

_____ 8. Riley played until she could barely move.

_____ 9. The director denied that he had stolen the idea for the movie.

_____ 10. Lake Superior, which is one of the Great Lakes, is the largest of the five.

_____ 11. The really bad news was that we couldn't go to the play.

Add an independent clause to each dependent clause to make a complete sentence.

12. who fell from the tree (adjective clause)

_____

13. that her dress was beautiful (noun clause)

_____

14. when the river rises above this point (adverb clause)

_____

Identifying Clauses

Underline each dependent clause and indicate if it is an adjective clause (**ADJ**), an adverb clause (**ADV**), or a noun (**N**) clause.

_____ 1. We didn't want to build a snowman that was like all the others.

_____ 2. We always do that before winter ends.

_____ 3. Today we would create a snowman that no one would forget.

_____ 4. What Craig thought of was perfect!

_____ 5. Build a giant snow monster is what we would do.

_____ 6. The monster grew quickly because the snow packed so well.

_____ 7. The neighbor who lives next door brought a six-foot ladder.

_____ 8. What became the monster's body were packed, giant snowballs.

_____ 9. He grew taller after we hoisted the second ball on top of the first.

_____ 10. To build his height, we added buckets of snow.

_____ 11. Since we were building a giant snow monster, we wanted him to be at least eight feet tall.

_____ 12. When the mound of snow was big enough, we carved out his face and his limbs.

_____ 13. When we stood back and looked, everyone agreed that he wasn't finished.

_____ 14. What he needed was sharp teeth and beady eyes.

_____ 15. Finally, we turned our snowy monster green by spraying him with colored water.

_____ 16. The snow monster that we put so much hard work into is a masterpiece.

_____ 17. The friend that lives down the street was a little scared of our creation.

_____ 18. We laughed when we saw his startled expression.

_____ 19. That our snow monster was unusual could not be denied.

_____ 20. I will never forget the day that we had so much fun.

Clause Review

Underline each noun clause and indicate whether the clause is being used as a subject (**S**), direct object (**DO**), indirect object (**IO**), object of a preposition (**OP**), or predicate noun (**PN**).

_____ 1. Frosted cookies are what make holidays delicious.

_____ 2. Whoever made this chocolate pie should be kissed.

_____ 3. I hope that this caramel corn isn't stale.

_____ 4. Maggie will give whoever says "please" a giant candy bar.

_____ 5. She was full after how much they ate.

Underline each adjective clause and circle the word it modifies.

6. We buy ice cream from the man who drives the ice-cream truck.

7. The honey that the bees make tastes great on toast.

8. His jawbreaker, which was the size of a golf ball, lasted a long time.

9. Dad and I get doughnuts at the bakery where my cousin works.

10. The fudge maker who worked in town was known for his delicious candy.

Underline each adverb clause and write the question it answers: **how**, **when**, **where**, or **why**.

_____ 11. You should brush your teeth whenever you've eaten sweets.

_____ 12. My brother is overexcited because he ate too much candy.

_____ 13. As winter progresses, we dip candy canes in melted chocolate.

_____ 14. We enjoy fondue by dipping strawberries in melted chocolate too.

_____ 15. Lisa and Michael shared a malted milkshake at the ice-cream parlor the opened recently.

Simple and Compound Sentences

A **simple sentence** contains one independent clause.

A **compound sentence** contains two independent clauses that are closely related. A comma and conjunction or a semicolon usually connects the two clauses.

    Mohammed is a sumo wrestler. (simple sentence)

    Mohammed trains very hard, but he has never won a competition. (compound sentence)

Identify each sentence as simple (**S**) or compound (**C**).

_____ 1. Sumo is the national sport of Japan.

_____ 2. There are six major sumo tournaments held each year in Japan, and they attract the attention of the entire nation.

_____ 3. In Japan, a tournament is called a basho.

_____ 4. A sumo ring measures 12 feet (3.66 m) in diameter and is made of sand and clay.

_____ 5. The goal in sumo wrestling is to either throw your opponent to the ground or to push him out of the ring.

_____ 6. Sumo has no weight classes for competition, and many wrestlers weigh more than 350 pounds (159 kg).

_____ 7. The wrestler's big stomach provides him with a low center of gravity, and it helps him withstand a charge by his opponent.

_____ 8. Every sumo competition begins with a special ceremony.

_____ 9. Before each match, the competitors throw salt into the ring to purify the ground, and they stamp their feet to crush evil.

_____ 10. The referee gives the signal, and the wrestlers take their position.

_____ 11. They crouch down and place both hands in front of them with their knuckles on the ground.

_____ 12. The highest rank in sumo wrestling is *yokozuna*; this means "grand champion."

Simple and Compound Sentences

A **simple sentence** contains one independent clause.

John walked into the center of town.

The train whistled past.

The doctor is in.

A **compound sentence** contains two independent clauses that are closely related. The clauses are often connected by a comma and conjunction or by a semicolon.

The team played hard, and they won the game easily.

Soccer is a low-scoring game, but it is very exciting.

The forward kicked the ball, and the goalie grabbed it.

Indicate whether each sentence is simple (**S**) or compound (**C**). Then, underline the simple subject and circle the simple predicate.

_____ 1. The Chartres Cathedral is a masterpiece of Gothic architecture, and it has become a famous landmark.

_____ 2. The town of Chartres is built on the bank of the Eure River.

_____ 3. Chartres is located in north-central France, and it is the capital of Eure-et-Loire.

_____ 4. The cathedral has two bell towers.

_____ 5. Cathedrals of this type were often the focal point of the community, and people sometimes devoted their entire lives to the construction of these religious buildings.

_____ 6. A fire in the year 1194 destroyed most of the cathedral, but it was rebuilt between 1194 and 1230.

Write a simple sentence and a compound sentence about other famous buildings.

7. (simple) _____

_____

8. (compound) _____

_____

Complex Sentences

A **complex sentence** contains one independent clause and one or more dependent clauses.

> (The independent clauses are underlined once; the dependent, twice.)
>
> The fish jumped over the dam when the wave crested.
>
> If you go to the store, buy me a candy bar.
>
> The carpenter who built this house is my brother.

Underline each independent clause once and each dependent clause twice.

1. The astronauts left the vehicle when the solar panel failed.

2. The United States became serious about space exploration when the Soviet Union launched *Sputnik I*.

3. If there is life on the moon, humans have not succeeded in finding it.

4. When a spacecraft is put in orbit, many people share the credit.

5. Yuri Gagarin, who was the first person to orbit the earth, died in 1968.

6. The Apollo program had a lunar module that was capable of landing on the moon and returning to the main vehicle.

7. The *Sputnik I*, which was launched in 1957, was the first artificial satellite.

8. When Neil Armstrong stepped onto the lunar surface, he was fulfilling a promise made by America's President Kennedy earlier in the decade.

9. The United States launched the space shuttle *Columbia*, which was the first reusable manned spacecraft.

10. The *Challenger*, which had seven astronauts on board, exploded in midair.

11. Because this disaster was so devastating, all American missions were temporarily stopped.

Write three complex sentences about space exploration.

12. _____

13. _____

14. _____

Compound/Complex Sentences

A **compound/complex sentence** contains two or more independent clauses and at least one dependent clause.

(The independent clauses are underlined once; the dependent clauses, twice.)

When the game was over, Seth took the ball, and Larry threw it into the stands.

Underline the independent clauses once and the dependent clauses twice.

1. If you have a solution, let us know, and we will try it.

2. Because Torika had studied previous chess matches, she was able to play brilliantly, and she beat Samia soundly.

3. When we get to the park, Austin will put up the tent, and Carla will start the fire.

4. Though the steak was not fully cooked, Jeremy cut it, and Isabella ate it.

5. Wallace had never gone to college, and he worked at the factory until he won a scholarship.

6. The food was free, and the people who came enjoyed it.

7. Though it was brand new, the stereo would not play, and it destroyed my tape.

8. Because Jennifer broke her arm, she could not play in the concert, and the orchestra sounded terrible.

9. Paige suggested the movie, and Elijah and Michael agreed when they heard her choice.

10. Stephen went back to Florida, where he opened a law firm, but it was not a financial success.

11. The enraged inventor sued the company, but when he finally won his case, he was deeply in debt.

Write three compound/complex sentences about your favorite book or movie.

12. _____

13. _____

14. _____

Sentence Structures

Identify each sentence as simple (**S**), compound (**C**), complex (**CX**), or compound/
complex (**C/CX**).

_____ 1. My grandma makes the best cheesy broccoli soup, and she serves it with
homemade bread.

_____ 2. Big chunks of potatoes make potato soup worth eating.

_____ 3. Even though I hate pea soup, my mom always makes it.

_____ 4. Chili tastes great on a cold winter day.

_____ 5. Because we eat soup every Saturday night, we try lots of kinds, and we
serve them in a variety of ways.

_____ 6. When we go out for Chinese food, we usually order egg drop soup.

_____ 7. A black bean soup with rice and tomato salsa on top is the best.

_____ 8. If you come over tonight, you may stay for dinner, and we will share our
minestrone.

_____ 9. Dad loves venison stew and whole wheat rolls.

_____ 10. Some people like clam chowder, but I'm not crazy about it.

_____ 11. When we're in a hurry, we just open a can of chicken noodle.

_____ 12. Kyle likes to eat at the Souper Bowl, where we go for soup and
sandwiches; he always orders their famous onion soup.

_____ 13. My mom and I are looking for new soup recipes.

_____ 14. When we find a recipe that looks good, we go shopping for ingredients,
and we make it the next day.

_____ 15. Some of our friends think we are strange because we love soup so much.

_____ 16. The new wedding soup recipe sounded delicious, but I did not like it at all.

_____ 17. Grandpa only likes soups that contain cheese or potatoes.

_____ 18. Dad wants to try to replicate a soup he ordered at a restaurant.

Recognizing Sentence Types

A **simple sentence** contains one independent clause. A c**ompound sentence** contains two independent clauses joined by a semicolon or a comma and a conjunction.

A **complex sentence** contains one independent clause and one or more dependent clauses.

A **compound/complex sentence** contains two or more independent clauses and at least one dependent clause.

Identify each sentence as simple (**S**), compound (**C**), complex (**CX**), or compound/complex (**C/CX**).

_____ 1. Whenever a new video game is developed, we immediately go to the store, and my mom looks it over carefully.

_____ 2. The car hit the tree, but there was no damage.

_____ 3. If the camping trip is cancelled, Jared will stay home, but Carla will probably go to a movie.

_____ 4. When you get to the store, you will be given a free gift.

_____ 5. The teacher, who tried to take charge, was very stern, but the class didn't pay much attention to him.

_____ 6. Kellie tried to get the pump started.

_____ 7. The disc jockey was on the air, and his replacement was waiting in the next room.

_____ 8. A city must be planned carefully, or people will not want to live in it.

_____ 9. We were going to attend the game, but it started raining.

_____ 10. I am going to do my homework after school, but I would rather play with my friends.

_____ 11. Shauna put a dollar into the pop machine, but nothing came out.

_____ 12. The book was exciting and easy to read.

_____ 13. Harry sang the song for his mom, and she loved it.

_____ 14. Because the computer was a very expensive purchase, Dad bought a special table for it, and he kept it in an air-conditioned room.

Sentences with Modifiers

> The complete subject or complete predicate of a sentence usually contains other words or phrases called **modifiers** that add to the meaning of the sentence.
>
> The <u>cold</u> water dripped <u>slowly over the jagged edge</u>.

Underline each subject modifier and circle each predicate modifier.

1. The small boy ran very fast.

2. The huge, gray dog ran eagerly.

3. The talented magician bowed gracefully.

4. The distraught mother silently watched.

5. The excited boy collided with the dog.

6. The long-stemmed roses landed in a tangled mess on the floor.

7. The frightened cat in the window jumped wildly.

Add modifiers to the simple subjects and predicates to create interesting sentences. Capitalize the first word of the sentence and add punctuation where needed.

8. player won game _____

9. car drove _____

10. children played _____

11. birds flew _____

12. Michelangelo painted murals _____

13. Miss Benally explained problem _____

14 sun shines _____

15. summer means _____

16. lakes freeze _____

17. trees grow _____

Misplaced Modifiers

Modifiers that are not placed near the word or phrase they modify are called **misplaced modifiers**.

Misplaced modifier: <u>Scared to death</u>, the dark night enveloped the lost student.

Correct: <u>Scared to death</u>, the lost student was enveloped by the dark night.

Underline the misplaced modifiers in the sentences. Then, rewrite each sentence correctly.

1. After school, I have a key for getting into our locked house.

    _____

2. Under the flowerpot, I always know I can find an extra key.

    _____

3. The flowerpot is missing unfortunately.

    _____

4. To let myself in, I consider breaking a window.

    _____

5. On the roof, I think about going down the chimney.

    _____

6. I sit on the porch and wait for my mom to get home for an hour.

    _____

7. We discover that the door had not even been locked when she arrives.

    _____

8. The dog barks at us as we go in through the window.

    _____

Dangling Modifiers

If a modifying word, phrase, or clause does not modify a word that is present in the sentence, it is called a **dangling modifier**. Every modifier must have a word that it clearly modifies.

Warmed by the sun, it felt good to be at the beach.

(**dangling modifier**—*Warmed by the sun* does not modify any word in the sentence.)

Warmed by the sun, we thought a day at the beach felt good.

(**correct**—*Warmed by the sun* modifies *we.*)

Underline each dangling modifier. If the modifier is used correctly, write **OK** in the blank.

_____ 1. While running down to the water, the sand was too hot.

_____ 2. Surrounded by a moat, I created a masterpiece.

_____ 3. Under the umbrella, the picnic basket filled with snack foods sat.

_____ 4. Reclining on the beach, sunscreen is extremely important.

_____ 5. With too much sun, many sunbathers will burn.

Rewrite each sentence to correct each dangling modifier.

6. Riding the big waves, excited shouts emerge from the water.

_____

7. Lying in the sun, my suntan lotion didn't work.

_____

8. Playing barefoot, the volleyball game took place on the hot sand.

_____

9. Tired and sandy, our beach day ended.

_____

10. Hanging out at the beach, the time was a lot of fun.

_____

Misplaced and Dangling Modifiers

Modifiers that are not placed near the words or phrases that they modify are called **misplaced modifiers**.

> **Misplaced modifier**: <u>Chilled to the bone</u>, the hot soup tasted good to the skiers.
>
> (Here *chilled to the bone* modifies the word *skiers* but is not placed near it.)

Underline each misplaced modifier. Then, write each sentence correctly.

1. The women's group is offering counseling for those who need it on Monday.

    _____

2. The new car was very popular with the race fans that raced past.

    _____

3. The company decided to buy a new building that needed more space.

    _____

4. The number increases every year of boating accidents.

    _____

> If a modifying word, phrase, or clause does not modify any particular word, then the modifier is called a **dangling modifier**. Every modifier must have a word that it clearly modifies.
>
> **Incorrect**: <u>Entering the bay</u>, the city loomed in front of us.
> (*Entering the bay* does not modify *city*.)
>
> **Correct**: <u>Entering the bay</u>, the boat began to head toward shore.
> (*Entering the bay* correctly modifies *the boat*.)

Underline each dangling modifier. If the modifier is used correctly, write **OK** in the blank.

_____ 5. Chilled by the snow, it felt good to be inside.

_____ 6. In the summer catalog, the models looked elegant.

_____ 7. Living on the beach all summer, the sunblock supply was quite low.

_____ 8. Startled by the wild animal, the scream caused me to whirl around suddenly.

Double Negatives

A **double negative** is an incorrect construction that uses two words when one is sufficient. Use only one negative word when you mean *no*.

  Incorrect: He did <u>not</u> do <u>nothing</u> all day. (two negative words)

  Correct: He did <u>not</u> do anything all day. (or) He did <u>nothing</u> all day. (one negative word)

Circle the negative words. Then, rewrite each sentence so that it does not contain a double negative construction.

1. I haven't got no time to wait for you.

    _____

2. You don't know nothing about the subject we're discussing.

    _____

3. You can't hardly find that tape anywhere.

    _____

4. Oprah said that she didn't want no one on the show with his attitude.

    _____

5. David couldn't hardly believe his good luck.

    _____

6. My brother doesn't do nothing all day long.

    _____

7. Gerardo hasn't never been to New York City before.

    _____

8. The police told the press that they would not have no further statements until Monday.

    _____

9. Penny didn't have nowhere to go, so she pouted.

    _____

Choppy Sentences

Choppy sentences are a series of short, closely related sentences that, if joined together, could be made into one smoother and less repetitive sentence.

choppy sentences: This book is interesting. It is a story about sumo wrestling. It is an exciting story.

corrected sentence: This book is an interesting and exciting story about sumo wrestling.

Rewrite each choppy sentence as a smooth, non-repetitive sentence.

1. In Japan, sumo wrestlers are considered living icons. They are heroes of their national sport.

   _____

   _____

2. Sumo wrestlers prefer to be extremely large. Wrestlers strive to get very fat.

   _____

   _____

3. A tournament lasts for 15 days. Wrestlers face a different opponent each day.

   _____

   _____

4. Wrestlers throw a handful of purifying salt. They must do this. They throw the salt before entering the hallowed ring.

   _____

   _____

5. The wrestling ring is considered a sacred place. It is called a dohyo.

   _____

   _____

6. Most matches are short. Most are intense. Most last less than one minute.

   _____

Correcting Fragments and Run-Ons

Rewrite the article below. Correct the run-ons, fragments, and choppy sentences.

Seeker's Thrill amusement park has just released news that the world's most state-of-the-art roller coaster, the new Monster Mile, is ready to roll. A select group of roller coaster enthusiasts will be the first to experience the ride since it is expected to be a sunny day at the park. The 100 special guests will strap in at 9:00 am and the ride will exceed record roller coaster speeds. Riders of the Monster Mile will stand during their 4.5-minute race through 15 corkscrew loops, dozens of turns, and a mile of coaster track and the other roller coasters will not be running until the park opens. The park will be open to the public at 12:00 noon and the rides will run until 11:00 pm, and parking will be free all day. Guests at Seeker's Thrill will be rewarded with a complimentary Monster Mile ice-cream bar after riding the thrilling roller coaster or some may choose no to ride the foreboding giant. Before leaving the park, however, anyone can purchase an "I survived the Monster Mile" T-shirt or hat then there will be a fireworks finale at 11:00 pm. Seeker's Thrill will close at midnight on its grand opening day so have a great time on "The Monster Mile"!

_____

_____

_____

_____

_____

_____

_____

_____

_____

_____

_____

Problem Verbs—Lie/Lay

Lie means to recline, to rest, or to remain in a reclining position. The principal forms of the verb *lie* are *lie, lay, (have/has/had) lain*. This verb never takes an object in any of its forms. There is no form of this verb ending in *-d*. *Lie* is sometimes confused with the verb *lay*, which means to put something down or to place something somewhere. Its principal forms are *lay, laid, (have/has/had) laid*. This verb always takes an object.

Examples of sentences using lie:

Joanna <u>lies</u> down for an hour every day.   (present)

Joanna <u>lay</u> on the deck in the sun.   (past)

Joanna <u>has lain</u> on the deck often.   (past participle)

Examples of sentences using lay:

Edgar <u>lays</u> linoleum for a department store.   (present)

Edgar <u>laid</u> linoleum all day.   (past)

Edgar <u>has laid</u> linoleum since he left high school.   (past participle)

Circle the correct verb in each sentences.

1. He (lay, laid) down to take a nap.

2. Linden has (lain, laid) carpet for that store for years.

3. Our dog (laid, lay) in the mud.

4. My aunt (lays, lies) on the sofa every morning.

5. The hen (laid, lay) an egg yesterday morning.

6. The injured animal (lay, laid) motionless.

7. I think I will (lay, lie) down and take a nap.

8. (Lay, Lie) that book down.

9. He had (lain, laid) the scissors on the table.

Use the verbs to write sentences.

10. lies (rests) _____

11. laid (put down) _____

12. lay (reclined) _____

Name_____

Problem Verbs—Sit/Set

The verb *sit* means to assume a sitting position or to occupy a seat. The principal forms of the verb *sit* are *sit, sat,* (*have/has/had*) *sat*. The verb *sit* never takes an object. This verb is sometimes confused with the verb *set*, which means to put something in position or to make something rigid. The principal forms of the verb *set* are *set, set,* (*have/has/had*) *set*. The verb *set* usually has an object.

Examples of sentences using sit:

I <u>sit</u> in the shade whenever I can.   (present)

Jack <u>sat</u> still, waiting for the fish to bite.   (past)

The governor <u>has sat</u> in that chair for many meetings.   (past participle)

Examples of sentences using set:

Tony <u>set</u> the silverware on the table.   (present)

Yesterday, Wallace <u>set</u> the clock after the storm.   (past)

The realtor <u>has set</u> his commission too high.   (past participle)

Circle the correct verb in each sentence.

1. He (set, sat) still while his hair was being cut.

2. You should always (sit, set) in good light when you read.

3. Grandpa likes to (sit, set) in the rocking chair.

4. We (set, sat) the correct time on the computer after the storm ended.

5. The little boy (set, sat) there looking depressed.

6. You may (sit, set) the book on the table.

7. Please (sit, set) here and relax while I try to find your book.

8. Let's (set, sit) here and watch the rain.

9. The boys (sat, set) on the roof.

Use the verbs to write sentences.

10. has set _____

11. sit _____

12. sat _____

Problem Verbs—Rise/Raise

The verb *rise* means to ascend, to swell up, and to gain value or force. The principal forms of the verb *rise* are *rise, rose, (have/has/had) risen*. The verb *rise* does not take an object. This verb is sometimes confused with the verb *raise*, which means to lift up something, to cause it to go up, to increase the amount, to collect a number of objects, or to breed and grow. Its principal parts are *raise, raised, (have/has/had) raised*. The verb *raise* always takes an object.

Examples of sentences using rise:

The sun rises in the east.   (present)

The rocket rose steadily into the atmosphere.   (past)

The tide had risen by morning.   (past participle)

Examples of sentences using raise:

Many farmers raise soybeans as a cash crop.   (present)

Shane raised the flag.   (past)

The charismatic politician had raised a huge sum of money.   (past participle)

Circle the correct verb in each sentence.

1. The hot air balloon (raises, rises) into the blue sky.

2. The stock market (rose, raised) 30 points yesterday because of the announcement.

3. The granite cliffs (raise, rise) high above the valley.

4. The guerilla leader (raised, rose) a great army of support.

5. The flood waters (raised, rose) rapidly.

6. The coffee dealers (rose, raised) the price of coffee beans.

7. The soldier (rose, raised) the flag.

8. The wedding guests had (raised, risen) their glasses for a toast.

Use the verbs to write sentences.

9. raise _____

10. rises _____

11. rose _____

12. had raised _____

Troublesome Verbs

Complete the chart with the missing verbs.

Present Tense	Past Tense	Past Participle
shake	shook	(have/has/had) shaken
lead		(have/has/had) led
freeze	froze	(have/has/had)
eat		(have/has/had) eaten
wear		(have/has/had) worn
know	knew	(have/has/had)
blow		(have/has/had) blown
drown	drowned	(have/has/had) drowned
catch	caught	(have/has/had)

Circle the correct verb in each sentence.

1. Kimberly (blow, blew) out the candles on her birthday cake.

2. You have (ate, eaten) all of the treats put out for the party.

3. What will you (wear, have worn) to the party tomorrow?

4. John (shook, shaked) his head.

5. I (knew, knowed) it was his birthday.

6. He (drowned, drownded) his burger with hot sauce.

7. I did not know to where the path (leaded, led).

8. The pond has been (froze, frozen) for several weeks now.

9. Terrance (catched, caught) a cold the day before the party.

10. I have (weared, worn) this dress before.

11. After an hour outside, the water in the pail had (frozen, froze).

Use the verbs to write sentences.

12. ate _____

13. lead _____

14. have shaken _____

More Troublesome Verbs

Complete the chart with the missing verbs.

Present Tense	Past Tense	Past Participle
become	became	(have/has/had) become
choose	chose	(have/has/had)
drink		(have/has/had) drunk
throw	threw	(have/has/had)
write	wrote	(have/has/had)
flow		(have/has/had) flowed
see	saw	(have/has/had)
swear		(have/has/had) sworn
climb		(have/has/had) climbed

Circle the correct verb in each sentence.

1. Ross has (swore, sworn) to tell the truth.

2. The rising river (flowed, flew) under the bridge.

3. Uma (wrote, written) many interesting letters.

4. Sam (become, became) angry yesterday.

5. Paul (has, have) climbed that tree in the backyard many times.

6. He (saw, see) that movie three times already.

7. I have (choosed, chosen) Michael to be on our team.

8. I (drunk, drank) all my milk, Mom!

9. The boy had (threw, thrown) the ball into the woods.

10. The knight (sweared, swore) his loyalty to the king.

11. Ruby has (became, become) a wonderful cook.

12. We found that the juice had (flew, flowed) from the hole in the cup.

Use the verbs to write sentences.

13. has seen _____

14. have written _____

More Troublesome Verbs

Complete the chart with the missing verbs.

Present Tense	Past Tense	Past Participle
cut	cut	(have/has/had) cut
drag		(have/has/had) dragged
wring	wrung	(have/has/had)
weave		(have/has/had) woven
lend	lent	(have/has/had)
say	said	(have/has/had)
take		(have/has/had) taken
let	let	(have/has/had)
go		(have/has/had) gone

Circle the correct verb in each sentence.

1. She has (wove, woven) a beautiful pattern into that garment.

2. Gabe (lent, lended) Jonathan a lot of money.

3. Byron (say, said) that he is not going to the game.

4. This whole thing has (taken, took) far too long already.

5. Ella (wrung, wringed) the water from the rag.

6. Grandpa (went, gone) to the store yesterday.

7. Eboni had (cut, cutted) the cake and grabbed a piece before anyone noticed.

8. We have (went, gone) to that restaurant before.

9. The gardener (drug, dragged) the heavy shrub to the truck.

Use the verbs to write sentences.

10. have gone _____

11. let _____

12. has lent _____

13. wrung _____

14. had said _____

Problem Pairs

There are certain pairs of words which are frequently confused. Some sound alike, some are spelled similarly, and some have similar meanings.

already—previously; **all ready**—totally prepared

altogether—entirely; **all together**—everyone in one group or place

its—possessive form of *it*; **it's**—contraction of *it is*

there—at that place; **their**—possessive form of *they*; **they're**—contraction of *they are*

than—conjunction used in comparisons; **then**—at that time

who's—contraction of *who is* or *who has*; **whose**—possessive form of *who*

Circle the correct word choice in each sentence.

1. (Whose, Who's) party did you attend?

2. We had (all ready, already) made the turn when we realized our mistake.

3. A reunion is a great time to get everyone (all together, altogether).

4. Leave that package (their, there) where you found it.

5. My team is much better (than, then) yours.

6. (Its, It's) just the way he plays the game.

7. (Whose, Who's) that student at the end of the hall?

8. We were (all ready, already) to go when we saw the flat tire.

9. We were not (all together, altogether) pleased with that book.

10. (Their, There) luggage was lost somewhere in the terminal.

11. If I pay for the tickets, (then, than) will you go?

12. (Their, They're) going to the baseball game.

13. (Its, It's) still raining.

14. The dog did not like (its, it's) collar.

15. I (already, all ready) have a dog.

16. I like tomato soup better (then, than) chicken noodle soup.

More Problem Pairs

Certain pairs of words are often confused. The best defense against making a mistake with these words is to check a dictionary.

brake—a mechanism for slowing down or stopping; **break**—to shatter or come apart

later—more late; **latter**—the second of two persons or things mentioned

lead—to go first, or a heavy metal; **led**—past tense of *lead*

loose—free, not tight; **lose**—to suffer the loss of

principal—head of a school, or important; **principle**—a rule of conduct, or a basic truth

plane—a flat surface, or an airplane; **plain**—not fancy, or a large area of flat land

Circle the correct word choice in each sentence.

1. The student driver missed the (break, brake) with his foot.

2. We will be going (later, latter) than you.

3. The room was lined with (led, lead) to protect the technician from the x-rays.

4. I went to the dentist because my tooth was (lose, loose).

5. The (principal, principle) works hard for her school.

6. She (led, lead) the way in the field of chemical engineering.

7. You don't have anything to (lose, loose).

8. I believe it is important to understand the (principle, principal) of gravity.

9. The glass will (break, brake) if you bump into it.

10. Henry thought that the (later, latter) of the two reasons made more sense.

11. The (plane, plain) was forced to make an emergency landing.

12. My tastes run to very (plain, plane) designs.

13. I will tell you about my problem (later, latter).

14. Follow these (principles, principals), and you will be a success.

15. The science students rolled the marble down the inclined (plain, plane).

Participles and Participial Phrases

A **participle** is a verb form that functions as an adjective. A **participial phrase** is a group of words that includes the participle and its related words.

The **present participle** is usually formed by adding *-ing* to the present tense verb.

Participle: The runner enjoyed the <u>cooling</u> breezes.

Participial phrase: <u>Cooling off</u>, the runners jumped into the pool.

The **past participle** is usually formed by adding *-ed* to the present tense verb. Check your dictionary for the way irregular verbs form the past participle.

Participle: Each <u>sunburned</u> person would be uncomfortable tonight.

Participial phrase: <u>Burned by the sun</u>, the teenager reached for a t-shirt.

Underline the participle and circle the word that it modifies.

1. We tiptoed around the sleeping child.

2. The surging river terrified the townspeople.

3. Each contestant auditioned her singing voice for the pageant.

4. The dried flowers were carefully hung in the barn.

5. The satisfied customers left the restaurant determined to come back.

6. The city removed the wrecked cars.

7. A watched pot never boils.

8. You could tell he was scared because of his shaking knees.

Underline each participial phrase and circle the word that it modifies.

9. Opening the door, Greg saw a huge crowd of people.

10. The car pictured in the brochure was a Toyota.

11. Donna saw a giraffe eating leaves.

12. Breathing hard, the runner collapsed.

13. The police, knocking loudly on the door, awakened everybody.

14. Entering the store, Evelyn walked down the center aisle.

15. Slipping into the water, the diver disappeared.

Participles

A **participle** is a verb form that functions as an adjective.

The **present participle** is usually formed by adding *-ing* to the present tense verb.

Rex barks at the <u>passing</u> cars.

The **past participle** is usually formed by adding *-ed* to the present tense verb.

A <u>determined</u> Rex tried to chase the car.

A **participial phrase** is a group of words that includes the participle and its objects, complements, or modifiers.

<u>Determined to succeed</u>, Rex chased the car.

Underline each participle and label it as present (**P**) or past (**PA**).

_____ 1. Romeo's parents inquire about their moping son.

_____ 2. Discovering Rosaline's name on the guest list, Benvolio encourages Romeo to "crash" the Capulet party.

_____ 3. Wearing a mask, Romeo arrives at the party.

_____ 4. There, he sees the smiling Juliet and longs to meet her.

_____ 5. The dancing couple fall hopelessly in love.

_____ 6. Struck by love, Juliet is distressed to learn that Romeo belongs to the house of Montague.

_____ 7. The feuding Montagues and Capulets hate each other.

_____ 8. Appearing on the balcony, Juliet declares her passion for Romeo.

_____ 9. Overheard by Romeo, her words of love inspire him.

_____ 10. Soon, a determined Romeo appeals to the friar to marry the couple immediately.

_____ 11. Standing before the friar, the young lovers are married in secret.

_____ 12. Committed to being reunited with her husband, Juliet carries out a dangerous plan.

_____ 13. Deceived by his sleeping wife, Romeo drinks the poison.

_____ 14. An awakening Juliet discovers her dying Romeo and tragically stabs herself to join him in death.

Infinitives and Infinitive Phrases

An **infinitive** is a present tense verb and is usually preceded by *to*. It is often used as a noun serving as a subject, a direct object, or a predicate noun.

To win the race is her goal.   (subject)

She hopes to win.   (direct object)

Ellen's goal is to win the race.   (predicate noun)

Underline each infinitive or infinitive phrase. Label each infinitive as a subject (**S**), direct object (**DO**), or predicate noun (**PN**).

_____ 1.   On a snowy day, I like to ski.

_____ 2.   To fish is all my grandpa ever wanted out of life.

_____ 3.   My father was hoping to play.

_____ 4.   Would you like to go?

_____ 5.   To debate is the reason that we are gathered here.

_____ 6.   To sleep was my only thought.

_____ 7.   One civic responsibility is to vote.

_____ 8.   I did not dare to speak.

_____ 9.   The purpose of talking is to communicate.

_____ 10.   The club's goal was to raise one thousand dollars.

_____ 11.   Ginny expected to pass the class with ease.

_____ 12.   Seth decided to go to the game by himself.

_____ 13.   To finish this paper by tomorrow will be very difficult.

_____ 14.   He did not dare to make the trip alone.

_____ 15.   To win a championship must be very exciting.

_____ 16.   Several people helped to rescue the boy.

_____ 17.   The teacher tried to show us several ways of solving the problem.

_____ 18.   Daysha wanted to have it all.

Gerunds and Gerund Phrases

A **gerund** is a verb form ending in *-ing* that functions as a noun. Gerunds are formed by adding *-ing* to the present tense verb form.

    <u>Painting</u> is my favorite hobby.

A **gerund phrase** is a group of words that includes a gerund and its related words.

    <u>Painting the ceiling</u> is a difficult job.

Underline each gerund and indicate if it is being used in the sentence as a subject (**S**), direct object (**DO**), object of preposition (**OP**), or predicate noun (**PN**).

_____ 1. Exercising is the best thing you can do for yourself.

_____ 2. My favorite hobby is skiing.

_____ 3. Dylan enjoys painting.

_____ 4. Cindy likes skating.

_____ 5. The tolling of the bells is getting on my nerves.

_____ 6. Whispering is not polite.

_____ 7. You can become a pro by practicing.

_____ 8. Jogging has become a very popular activity.

Underline each gerund phrase and indicate its use in the sentence (**S**, **DO**, **OP**, or **PN**).

_____ 9. Shannette was soon bored with reading her book.

_____ 10. Vanessa enjoys reading historical novels.

_____ 11. Flipping hamburgers is a good way to make some money.

_____ 12. The referee began by introducing the players to one another.

_____ 13. Drinking a lot of water is good for you.

_____ 14. Quan's new task is collecting newspapers to recycle.

_____ 15. Asking questions is probably the best way to learn something.

_____ 16. Playing baseball is my idea of an enjoyable afternoon.

Gerunds

A **gerund** is a verb form ending in *–ing* that functions as a noun. Gerunds are formed by adding *–ing* to the present tense verb form. A **gerund phrase** is a group of words that includes a gerund and its related words.

Underline Dancing is my favorite form of exercise. (gerund)

Underline Dancing the polka is a good workout. (gerund phrase)

Underline each gerund or gerund phrase and indicate if it is being used as a subject (**S**), direct object (**DO**), object of a preposition (**OP**), or predicate noun (**PN**).

_____ 1. Cleaning is the worst job.

_____ 2. I prefer cooking.

_____ 3. Sometimes I avoid my chores by complaining.

_____ 4. Another strategy is procrastinating.

_____ 5. Vacuuming isn't so bad.

_____ 6. I hate dusting.

_____ 7. Occasionally, the windows need washing.

_____ 8. Mopping makes the floors shine.

_____ 9. My room appears messy when the bed needs making.

_____ 10. Mowing the lawn can be relaxing work.

_____ 11. I'm not fond of pulling weeds when it is scorching hot outside.

_____ 12. Washing dishes is a job my sister and I share.

_____ 13. A disgusting chore is scrubbing the toilet.

_____ 14. We never worry about polishing the silver.

_____ 15. Feeding the cat has been my little brother's only chore.

_____ 16. Everyone in our house is responsible for folding laundry.

_____ 17. Dad mainly likes fixing things.

_____ 18. The best part of a chore is finishing the job.

Verbals: Review

Verbals (participles, gerunds, and infinitives) are verb forms that do not perform as verbs. Instead, they function as other parts of speech.

Underline each verbal phrase and indicate whether it is a participial phrase (**P**), a gerund phrase (**G**), or an infinitive phrase (**I**).

_____ 1. He was asked to buy some fresh vegetables.

_____ 2. Known as one of the best pitchers in baseball, Warren Spahn was inducted into the Hall of Fame.

_____ 3. Kelly practices juggling three apples at a time.

_____ 4. Lola tried to study on a regular basis.

_____ 5. It is important to exercise every day.

_____ 6. Talking to himself, my brother walked down the street.

_____ 7. Xander volunteered to have everybody over for dinner.

_____ 8. Taking a vitamin is the way he starts his day.

_____ 9. Standing up to his knees in the water, Wesley cast his fly into the river.

_____ 10. The boys all want to go to the amusement park.

_____ 11. Exhausted from the long journey, the fish wallowed in the shallow water.

_____ 12. Hooking rugs is a very interesting hobby for many.

_____ 13. The principal, depressed by the poor attendance, worked on a new plan.

_____ 14. Baking cookies helps relieve my tension.

_____ 15. Anne likes painting seashells.

Write sentences using the following verb forms.

16. (participial) _____

17. (gerund) _____

18. (infinitive) _____

Name_____

Active Voice Verbs

A verb is in the **active voice** when the subject is performing the action.

(The subject is underlined once; the verb, twice.)

Ron changed his clothes.

The elephant fell from the stand.

The stone shattered his glasses.

Underline each simple subject once and each active voice verb twice.

1. Amelia Earhart flew alone over the Atlantic Ocean.

2. She made her crossing in 1932.

3. Amelia opened the field of aviation for many other women.

4. Ms. Earhart worked as a nurse's aide during World War I.

5. She earned a pilot's license by 1922.

6. She married George Putnam, a publisher.

7. This brave pilot tried to fly around the world in 1937.

8. Her plane disappeared during a flight over the Pacific Ocean.

9. Her mysterious disappearance fueled much speculation over the years.

10. Some people believe she drowned.

11. Her navigator also vanished.

Write five sentences using active verbs about a trip you have taken or would like to take. Underline the simple subjects once and the active verbs twice.

12. _____

13. _____

14. _____

15. _____

16. _____

Active Voice

A verb is in the **active voice** when the subject of the sentence is performing the action.
Hayden <u>likes</u> raising chickens.

Circle each active voice verb.

Hen's eggs take just 21 days to hatch. The hen must sit on her eggs to keep them warm until the chicks are born. Inside the egg, yolk and white provide nourishment for the bird. A red spot on the yolk will grow into a chick after three weeks. Tiny organs form, such as a beak and a stomach. The wings and feet develop too. Sticky feathers cover the chick, and the chick's egg tooth forms. Tiny holes in the egg's shell allow air to pass in and out. The chick's head lies near an air pocket at one end of the egg. The chick pushes its beak into the pocket to get its first breath of air. The chick uses its sharp egg tooth to break out of its shell. Finally, the baby bird dries and fluffs its yellow feathers and begins its search for food. As an adult, a chicken's weight ranges from about 1.1 pounds (0.5 kg) to more than 11 pounds (5 kg). Feathers, which cover most of the body, will keep the chicken warm in cold weather. A chicken's feathers also come in a range of patterns. Unlike some other birds, chickens develop fleshy structures called the comb and wattle. These structures help keep the chicken cool and help in recognition. The shape and size of the comb vary from breed to breed.

Passive Voice Verbs

A verb is in the **passive voice** when the subject is receiving the action.

    (The subject is underlined once; the verb, twice.)

    The windows were cleaned by Roger.

    The house was painted by professionals.

    A lot of homework was given by the teacher.

Rewrite the sentences to use active voice verbs instead of passive voice verbs.

1. The people of France had been ruled by the aristocracy for centuries.

   _____

2. Louis XVI was blamed by the common people for new, burdensome taxes.

   _____

3. In 1789, a royal fortress called the Bastille was stormed by a mob of angry Parisians.

   _____

4. Royal troops were forced by the mob to withdraw from Paris.

   _____

5. Later, the French government was overthrown by Napoleon Bonaparte.

   _____

6. The central government was made strong through Napoleon's efficient administration.

   _____

7. Europe was nearly destroyed by Napoleon's ambition.

   _____

8. Napoleon was finally defeated by his enemies at the Battle of Waterloo.

   _____

9. The rest of Europe also was influenced by the French Revolution.

   _____

Passive Voice

A verb is in the **passive voice** when the subject is receiving the action.

Sweets <u>are loved</u> by cultures all over the world.

Underline the passive voice verbs. Then, rewrite each sentence using the active voice.

1. Tamarind (tam-uh-rind) is a brown, sticky treat from the tamarind pod, which is eaten by children in India.

   _____

   _____

2. Tamarillos (tam-uh-RILL-oze) are tangy, red or yellow, football-shaped fruits that are enjoyed by New Zealanders.

   _____

   _____

3. In the Caribbean, a sweet treat called sugar cane is enjoyed by many.

   _____

   _____

4. In South America, green, heart-shaped cherimoyas (chair-ee-MOY-yuz) are favored by the children of Chile.

   _____

   _____

5. A sweet and crunchy brown root, called jicama (hee-kuh-mah), is served by the people of Mexico.

   _____

   _____

6. The breadfruit, a tropical fruit that tastes like baked bread, has been made a favorite by natives of the Pacific Islands.

   _____

   _____

Active and Passive Voice

Identify the voice of each verb by labeling it as active (**A**) or passive (**P**). If the verb is in passive voice, rewrite the sentence using a verb in the active voice.

_____ 1. The scavenger hunt game was played by the entire class.

_____

_____

_____ 2. The class was divided into two teams by Mr. McDonough, our homeroom teacher.

_____

_____

_____ 3. We called our team "The Scavengers."

_____

_____

_____ 4. The other team gave themselves the name "The Search Party."

_____

_____

_____ 5. All of the clues were carefully hidden by our teacher.

_____

_____

_____ 6. At the beginning of he game, each team was given the first clue by Mr. McDonough.

_____

_____

_____ 7. After a long and challenging hunt for clues, the game was finally won by "The Search Party."

_____

_____

Using Active and Passive Voice Verbs

A verb is in the **active voice** when the subject performs the action. A verb is in the **passive voice** when the subject receives the action.

Passive voice should be used sparingly. Active voice expresses action in a natural, more direct way.

Identify the voice of each verb by labeling it as active (**A**) or passive (**P**). If the verb is in passive voice, rewrite the sentence using a verb in the active voice.

_____ 1. The pharaohs constructed many temples in honor of the Egyptian gods.

_____

_____ 2. The Egyptians were conquered by the Hyksos.

_____

_____ 3. The Hyksos used horses and chariots to defeat the Egyptian army.

_____

_____ 4. The Egyptians learned to use the same tactics and drove the Hyksos out.

_____

_____ 5. The course of Egyptian history was changed by Amenhotep IV.

_____

_____ 6. He worshipped a sun god called the Aton.

_____

_____ 7. The Aton was represented as the disk of the sun.

_____

_____ 8. The capital of Egypt was moved to Akhetaton by the king.

_____

_____ 9. Several other changes by the king angered many Egyptians.

_____

Imperative Mood

The mood of the verb indicates the attitude or viewpoint behind the verb's expression. The **imperative mood** indicates a command or a request. The subject is always *you,* though this is rarely expressed.

Please, close the door. (*You* is understood to be the subject of this sentence.)

Use the verbs to write sentences in the imperative mood.

1. check _____

2. return _____

3. wash _____

4. deliver _____

5. develop _____

6. count _____

7. drive _____

8. climb _____

9. send _____

10. take _____

Write three sentences in the imperative mood that you might hear your principal or teacher say. Underline the verbs.

11. _____

12. _____

13. _____

Write (**I**) by each sentence written in the imperative mood.

_____ 14. The boy threw the baseball.

_____ 15. Sit here, please.

_____ 16. That movie was thoroughly enjoyable.

_____ 17. Pass the paper to me.

_____ 18. I love to paint.

_____ 19. The windows need to be washed.

Imperative Mood

The mood of the verb indicates the attitude or viewpoint behind the verb's expression. The **imperative mood** indicates a command or a request. The subject is always *you*, though this is rarely expressed.

Please wake me up at 7:00.

Make up your mind.

Write (**Y**) in the space if the sentence uses the imperative mood. Write (**N**) if it does not.

_____ 1. Mow the lawn.

_____ 2. Quiet down, please.

_____ 3. She dances gracefully.

_____ 4. The pizza is hot.

_____ 5. Go outside to play.

_____ 6. The flowers smell nice.

_____ 7. Wait for me!

_____ 8. Mustard tastes gross.

_____ 9. Just behave yourself.

_____ 10. Please pass the salt.

_____ 11. He's coming home now.

_____ 12. Take the garbage out.

For each riddle, write your own answer using the imperative mood.

13. What did the tired light say?

_____

14. What did the whistling teapot say?

_____

15. What did the chicken's mother say before he crossed the road?

_____

Introductory Phrases and Clauses

Use a comma to separate an **introductory phrase or clause** from the rest of the sentence. The phrases often contain a preposition.

<u>Because I am sick</u>, I will not be able to attend the medieval festival at the park.

Underline the introductory phrase or clause in each sentence. Then, add the proper punctuation.

1. During the Middle Ages the European form of government was feudalism.

2. At that time in European history there were many fiefs, or estates of feudal lords.

3. In return for his loyalty a nobleman was provided with land by the king.

4. Under the feudal system the owner of a fief was often a lord whose land was inhabited by people who promised to serve him.

5. When a person controlled land he also had political, economic, judicial, and military power.

6. At the age of about seven many young boys left home to train for knighthood.

7. As soon as a squire had mastered the necessary skills he became a knight.

8. As a knight a nobleman was a soldier for the king when necessary.

9. Because they had few rights peasants were at the mercy of their lords.

10. In return for clerical services many lords gave fiefs to the church.

Write an introductory phrase or clause for each sentence. Add the proper punctuation.

11. _____ preparations for the feast began.

12. _____ the manor had to be cleaned.

13. _____ large amounts of elaborate foods were prepared.

14. _____ trumpets announced the arrival of the king.

15. _____ all the guests enjoyed a feast fit for a king.

Comma Use

A comma is used to set off an introductory phrase or dependent clause.

   When you get home, we'll go to the mall.

A comma is used after words of direct address at the beginning of the sentence.

   Michael, call me when you get home.

A comma is used after introductory words such as *yes, indeed, well, in addition, thus,* and *moreover.*

   Yes, I agree with you completely.

   Thus, the game ended before it had begun.

Use two commas to set off interrupting words or expressions.

   Have you, by the way, ordered lunch yet?

Add commas where needed.

1. When I graduate from high school I plan to go to college.

2. Yes that is a good idea.

3. Of course you will need good grades to get into the college of your choice.

4. Seeing that you are a good student I know you'll have no problem.

5. In addition your involvement in extracurricular activities is important.

6. Travis what will you be studying in college?

7. If I get there I'd like to study oceanography.

8. Well you will have your work cut out for you.

9. You will find I'm sure that it is a competitive field.

10. Indeed it won't be easy.

11. Jack how about you?

12. I would like I think to go to medical school.

13. Fortunately I've been studying hard all year.

Comma Practice

Add commas where needed in the phone messages below.

1. Hi call me when you get home. I will I think be home all evening.

2. Greg this is cousin Hugo. We miss you! In addition to that I have something exciting to tell you.

3. Since you're not home yet I think I'll go shopping without you. By the way I did find your bracelet. It was on the counter next to the sink. If you can't come get it I will put it in the mail.

4. Mom I went to Scott's. Yes I already did all of my English homework. I will be home for dinner of course especially since it's spaghetti night.

5. Laura I received your request. For more information please write to us at the Venezuela Tourist Association.

6. Hello is this the Lewis residence? Your dog I believe is running loose on Jasper Court. If we can we will lure him into our backyard to keep him safe until you're back.

7. Don't forget your dentist appointment Mr. Dolby at 11:00 tomorrow morning. If you can't make it please call and cancel as soon as possible.

8. This is Rebecca your niece calling at 5:00 pm. If you still need a babysitter for Friday night I can do it. Just give me a call I guess whenever you get home.

9. This is Mom calling to remind you to take out the trash before it gets dark. Oh and don't forget to brush your teeth before you go to bed.

10. I'm calling on behalf of the Cristoffer Foundation which is a non-profit organization that helps children in need. Please don't forget us this year. As you know our children are counting on you.

Prefixes

Words are created using three kinds of parts. Prefixes, suffixes, and roots are named according to their location in words.

Prefixes are added at the beginning of words. Add the prefix *pre-* (meaning *before*) to the word *view* to create the word *preview*, meaning to see early or beforehand.

Match each prefix with a root word to form a new word.

_____	1. anti	A. merge		_____	11. post	K. eager
_____	2. tele	B. claim		_____	12. bi	L. hero
_____	3. sub	C. call		_____	13. co	M. sound
_____	4. under	D. live		_____	14. mini	N. clockwise
_____	5. pro	E. ordinary		_____	15. over	O. cycle
_____	6. en	F. cover		_____	16. extra	P. ordinary
_____	7. re	G. freeze		_____	17. super	Q. violent
_____	8. out	H. courage		_____	18. non	R. author
_____	9. extra	I. meter		_____	19. ultra	S. skirt
_____	10. peri	J. phone		_____	20. counter	T. war

Choose combined words from above and use them to write sentences.

21. _____

22. _____

23. _____

24. _____

25. _____

Recognizing Nouns: Suffixes

A word ending is called a **suffix**. The following suffixes are sometimes used to end nouns: -hood, -dom, -ment, -ance, -ness, -er, and -or.

childhood, earldom, excitement, appearance, illness, teacher, animator

Use a suffix to create a noun from each of the words below.

1. drive _____

2. adult _____

3. neighbor _____

4. free _____

5. still _____

6. sick _____

7. govern _____

8. attend _____

9. king _____

10. parent _____

11. firm _____

12. happy _____

13. amuse _____

14. bore _____

15. sing _____

16. encourage _____

Circle the suffix in each of the nouns below. Write a sentence for each of the nouns.

17. statehood

_____

18. insurance

_____

19. player

_____

20. operator

_____

21. establishment

_____

Answer Key

Page 5
1. we; 2. living, midwest; 3. the; 4. if; 5. latin american; 6. some, south; 7. there, bible; 8. the, talmud; 9. Answers will vary. 10. Answers will vary. 11. Answers will vary. 12. Answers will vary. 13. Answers will vary.

Page 6
1. red, sea; 2. battle, midway, world, war; 3. senator, javits; 4. big, ben, london; 5. parliament; 6. white, house; 7. associated, press; 8. Answers will vary. 9. Answers will vary. 10. Answers will vary. 11. Answers will vary.

Page 7
1. English, chemistry, dad, aunt, sarah, grandma, uncle, Umberto, good, housekeeping, the, drummer, boy, shiloh, the, oxford, english, dictionary, stopping, by, woods, snowy, evening, much, ado, nothing; 2. Answers will vary. 3. Answers will vary. 4. Answers will vary. 5. Answers will vary. 6. Answers will vary. 7. Answers will vary. 8. Answers will vary.

Page 8
1. thing; 2. person; 3. place; 4. thing; 5. person; 6. thing; 7. place; 8. thing; 9. thing; 10. idea; 11. person; 12. thing; 13. idea; 14. place; 15. idea; 16. idea; 17. a; 18. an; 19. a; 20. an; 21. a; 22. a; 23. a; 24. a; 25. an; 26. a; 27. an; 28. an; 29. Answers will vary.

Page 9
1. Answers will vary. 2. Answers will vary. 3. Answers will vary. 4. Answers will vary. 5. Answers will vary. 6. Answers will vary. 7. Answers will vary. 8. Answers will vary. 9. Answers will vary. 10. Answers will vary. 11. Answers will vary. 12. Answers will vary. 13. Answers will vary. 14. Answers will vary. 15. Answers will vary. 16. Answers will vary. 1–16. Check that proper nouns are circled. 17. Answers will vary.

Page 10
1. C; 2. A; 3. C; 4. A; 5. C; 6. C; 7. C; 8. C; 9. C; 10. A; 11. A; 12. C; 13. (circled) Mount Everest, Tibet, mountain, Earth; 14. (circled) nomads; (underlined) energy, struggle; 15. (underlined) skill, horsemanship; 16. (circled) monk, people; (underlined) honor; 17. (circled) Dalai Lama, leader, people; (underlined) inspiration; 18. (circled) Tibet, monasteries; (underlined) today, past; 19. (circled) monks, monasteries; (underlined) education, art, worship; 20. Answers will vary.

Page 11
1. Answers will vary. 2. Answers will vary. 3. Answers will vary. 4. Answers will vary. 5. Answers will vary. 6. Answers will vary. 7. Answers will vary. 8. Answers will vary. 9. Answers will vary. 10. Answers will vary. 11. Answers will vary. 12. Answers will vary.

Page 12
1. monkeys; 2. classes; 3. taxes; 4. berries; 5. loaves; 6. latches; 7. fezzes; 8. wishes; 9. hooves; 10. galleys; 11. horses; 12. roofs; 13. puffs; 14. honeys; 15. colors; 16. waltzes; 17. wives; 18. victories; 19. potatoes; 20. tresses; 21. crises; 22. brothers-in-law; 23. men; 24. oxen; 25. spoonfuls; 26. data

Page 13
1. woman's; 2. mice's; 3. horses'; 4. girls'; 5. teacher's; 6. umbrella's; 7. princess'; 8. home's; 9. players'; 10. students'; 11. host's; 12. presidents'; 13. scissors'; 14. Schindler's; 15. leaves'; 16. witnesses'; 17. actress'; 18. statue's; 19. pants'; 20. river's; 21. company's; 22. nurse's; Answers will vary.

Page 14
1. S; 2. S, is; 3. S, was; 4. S, its; 5. P, their; 6. S, is; 7. S, is; 8. S; 9. P, are, their; 10. P, were, their; Answers will vary.

Page 15
1. (circled) became, (underlined) consultant; 2. (circled) was, (underlined) storyteller; 3. (circled) is, (underlined) student; 4. (circled) was, (underlined) president; 5. (circled) is, (underlined) capital; 6. (circled) is, (underlined) poem; 7. (circled) became, (underlined) authority; 8. (circled) is, (underlined) commander; 9. (circled) became, (underlined) member; 10. (circled) was, (underlined) sculptor; 11. (circled) became, (underlined) carpenter; 12. (circled) is, (underlined) chairperson; 13. (circled) was, (underlined) leader; 14. (circled) was, (underlined) soldier; 15. Answers will vary. 16. Answers will vary. 17. Answers will vary. 18. Answers will vary.

Page 16
1. 3; 2. 2; 3. 1; 4. 3; 5. 1; 6. 3; 7. 3; 8. 2; 9. 3; 10. 1; 11. Answers will vary. 12. Answers will vary. 13. Answers will vary.

Page 17
1. 1: We; 2. 2: you, 1: we; 3. 3: She, her; 4. 3: she, her; 5. 2: you, you; 6. 3: she, she; 7. 3: he, her; 8. 3: They, she; 9. 3: She, them; 10. 3: she; 11. 3: They, she, her; 12. 1: We, 3: her; 13. Answers will vary. 14. Answers will vary. 15. Answers will vary.

Page 18
1. likes; 2. is; 3. is; 4. were; 5. deserves; 6. has; 7. plays; 8. are; 9. were; 10. is; 11. is; 12. wish; 13. were; 14. have; 15. has

Page 19
1. Her; 2. My, her; 3. His; 4. their; 5. its; 6. their; 7. Our; 8. hers; 9. theirs; 10. Our; 11. Who; 12. Which; 13. What; 14. whom; 15. Whose; 16. Answers will vary. 17. Answers will vary.

Page 20
1. myself; 2. yourself; 3. himself; 4. ourselves; 5. yourselves; 6. herself; 7. herself; 8. (circled) that, (underlined) includes fruit; 9. (circled) who, (underlined) eat a good breakfast; 10. (circled) whom, (underlined) I have put my trust; 11. (circled) that, (underlined) I must follow; 12. (circled) who, (underlined) always eats healthy foods; 13. (circled) which, (underlined) I started last night; 14. (circled) who, (underlined) is very slender; 15. (circled) who, (underlined) has to watch everything I eat

Page 21
1. I: N, S; she: F, S; 2. It: N, S; 3. you: N, S; me: N, S; we: N, P; 4. we: N, P; it: N, S; 5. He: M, S; 6. We: N, P; I: N, S; it: N, S; 7. he: M, S; 8. you: N, S; you: N, S; 9. it; 10. it; 11. they/them; 12. they/them; 13. they/them; 14. it; 15. it; 16. they/them; 17. they/them; 18. it

Page 22
1. probe, A; 2. strips, A; 3. adjust, A; 4. is, L; 5. is, L; 6. contains, A; 7. is, L; 8. is, L; 9. A; 10. L; 11. A; 12. A; 13. L; 14. A; 15. L; 16. A; 17. A; 18. A; 19. L; 20. L; 21. Answers will vary; 22. Answers will vary; 23. Answers will vary; 24. Answers will vary; 25. Answers will vary; 26. Answers will vary

Page 23
1. are, L; 2. are, L; 3. are, L; 4. eat, A; 5. screams, A; 6. is, L; 7. is, L; 8. live, A; 9. are, A; 10. tame, A; 11. are, L; 12. fly, A; 13. nest, A; 14. are, L; 15. live, A; Paragraphs will vary.

Page 24
1. crawled, crawled; 2. skated, skated; 3. fished, fished; 4. climbed, climbed; 5. loved, loved; 6. answered, answered; 7. traveled, traveled; 8. contended, contended; 9. pretended, pretended; 10. developed, developed; 11. Answers will vary.

Answer Key

12. Answers will vary. 13. Answers will vary. 14. Answers will vary. 15. Answers will vary. 16. Answers will vary. 17. Answers will vary. 18. Answers will vary.

Page 25
1. froze, frozen; 2. broke, broken; 3. fought, fought; 4. became, become; 5. saw, seen; 6. shook, shaken; 7. gave, given; 8. ate, eaten; 9. took, taken; 10. wore, worn; 11. Answers will vary. 12. Answers will vary. 13. Answers will vary. 14. Answers will vary. 15. Answers will vary. 16. Answers will vary.

Page 26
1. (underlined) is, (circled) Water, part; 2. (underlined) are, (circled) molecules, simple; 3. (underlined) is, (circled) management, problem; 4. (underlined) is, (circled) desert, region; 5. (underlined) is, (circled) living, common; 6. (underlined) is, (circled) farming, restricted; 7. (underlined) is, (circled) rainfall, scarce; 8. (underlined) is, (circled) water, difficult; 9. (underlined) are, (circled) states, desperate; 10. (underlined) are, (circled) rivers, sources; 11. (underlined) is, (circled) It, important; 12. (underlined) are, (circled) areas, cold; 13. (underlined) are, (circled) deserts, hot; 14. (underlined) is, (circled) desert, Sahara; 15. Answers will vary. 16. Answers will vary. 17. Answers will vary. 18. Answers will vary.

Page 27
1. (underlined) remains, (circled) lion, sight; 2. (underlined) is, (circled) puma, lion; 3. (underlined) looked, (circled) lioness, powerful; 4. (underlined) becomes, (circled) puma, secretive; 5. (underlined) became, (circled) panther, nuisance; 6. (underlined) seemed, (circled) extinction, possible; 7. (underlined) became, (circled) environmentalists, interested; 8. (underlined) is, (circled) puma, animal; 9. (underlined) became, (circled) information, crucial; 10. (underlined) is, (circled) puma, plentiful; 11. Answers will vary. 12. Answers will vary. 13. Answers will vary. 14. Answers will vary. 15. Answers will vary. 16. Answers will vary.

Page 28
1. (underlined) cast, (circled) fire, shadows; 2. (underlined) bought, (circled) choir, outfits; 3. (underlined) hit, (circled) rails, roof; 4. (underlined) handled, (circled) Roberto, torch; 5. (underlined) picked, (circled) jockey, song; 6. (underlined) hit, (circled) outfielder, wall; 7. (underlined) stopped, (circled) goalie, ball; 8. (underlined) jumped, (circled) horse, obstacle; 9. (underlined) slugged, (circled) Kenyon, baseball; 10. (underlined) served, (circled) he, ball; 11. (underlined) painted, (circled) woman, room; 12. (underlined) washed, (circled) Chrissie, windows; 13. (underlined) types, (circled) friend, words; 14. (underlined) slammed, (circled) toddler, drawer; 15. Answers will vary. 16. Answers will vary. 17. Answers will vary. 18. Answers will vary.

Page 29
1. (circled) city, (underlined) is located; 2. (circled) control, (underlined) has changed; 3. (circled) city, (underlined) was captured; 4. (circled) city, (underlined) flourished; 5. (circled) it, (underlined) was sacked; 6. (circled) Temple of Jerusalem, (underlined) was built; 7. (circled) Temple, (underlined) was destroyed; 8. (circled) people, (underlined) gather; 9. (circled) mosque, (underlined) was built; 10. (circled) place, (underlined) stands; 11. (circled) Jerusalem, (underlined) is revered; 12. (circled) tensions, (underlined) have arisen; 13. (circled) plans, (underlined) have failed; 14. (circled) signs, (underlined) are printed; 15. (circled) Pilgrims, (underlined) come; 16. Answers will vary. 17. Answers will vary. 18. Answers will vary. 19. Answers will vary.

Page 30
1. F, Answers will vary. 2. PA, Answers will vary. 3. PA, Answers will vary. 4. P, Answers will vary. 5. F, Answers will vary. 6. PA, Answers will vary. 7. Answers will vary. 8. Answers will vary. 9. Answers will vary.

Page 31
1. (underlined) was born, (circled) was; 2. (underlined) was raised, (circled) was; 3. (underlined) was introduced, (circled) was; 4. (underlined) are attracted, (circled) are; 5. (underlined) has been refined, (circled) has, been; 6. (underlined) was exploring, (circled) was; 7. (underlined) had studied, (circled) had; 8. (underlined) was forming, (circled) was; 9. (underlined) was supported, (circled) was; 10. (underlined) was convinced, (circled) was; 11. (underlined) was fascinated, (circled) was; 12. (underlined) was strengthened, (circled) was; 13. (underlined) has had, (circled) has had; 14. (underlined) have opposed, (circled) have; 15. (underlined) have referred, (circled) have; 16. Answers will vary. 17. Answers will vary. 18. Answers will vary. 19. Answers will vary.

Page 32
1. mangy (1), old (1), long (1); 2. warm (1), blazing (1); 3. cold (1); 4. bright (1), red (1), stocking (1), big (1); 5. cold (1), red (1), blinding (1); 6. those (3), majestic (1), heavy (1); 7. tiny (1), four (2); 8. two (2), icy (1); 9. pitiful (1); 10. bitter (1); 11. warm (1); 12. safe (1), peaceful (1), toasty (1); 13. several (2), thick (1), wool (1), roaring (1); 14. next (3), long (1), warm (1), spring (1); 15. faithful (1), bushy (1); 16. Answers will vary. 17. Answers will vary. 18. Answers will vary.

Page 33
1. dominant, land; 2. Greek, terrible; 3. gigantic; 4. large, flesh; 5. herbivorous; 6. earlier, primitive, small, reptile-like; 7. huge; 8. sudden; 9. temperature; 10. geological, food; 11. thrilling, amazing; 12. blood-curdling, favorite, dinosaur; 13. Answers will vary. 14. Answers will vary. 15. Answers will vary. 16. Answers will vary. 17. Answers will vary.

Page 34
1. stormier; 2. harder; 3. stronger; 4. flimsier; 5. more sturdy; 6. more dismal; 7. larger; 8. younger; 9. louder; 10. calmer; 11. Answers will vary. 12. Answers will vary. 13. Answers will vary. 14. Answers will vary.

Page 35
1. greatest; 2. most glamorous, most exotic; 3. tallest; 4. most difficult; 5. most intricate; 6. most talented; 7. nastiest; 8. weakest; 9. silliest; 10. Answers will vary. 11. Answers will vary. 12. Answers will vary. 13. Answers will vary.

Page 36
1. best; 2. farther; 3. better; 4. worst; 5. most; 6. less; 7. least; 8. Answers will vary. 9. Answers will vary. 10. Answers will vary.

Page 37
1. a; 2. an; 3. an; 4. a; 5. a; 6. a; 7. a; 8. an; 9. an; 10. an; 11. an; 12. a; 13. a; 14. a; 15. a; 16. a; 17. (circle) the, the (underline) fifty-five; 18. (circle) A (underline) two-hundred; 19. (underline) five; 20. (circle) the (underline) Twenty; 21. (circle) the (underline) one; 22. (circle) The (underline) twenty-three; 23. (circle) the (underline) ten; 24. Answers will vary. 25. Answers will vary. 26. Answers will vary. 27. Answers will vary. 28. Answers will vary.

Page 38
1. these; 2. that; 3. that; 4. that; 5. those; 6. this; 7. that; 8. that; 9. those; 10. these; 11. That; 12. These, those; 13. This; 14. That,

Answer Key

that; 15. Some, many; 16. Few; 17. Several; 18. Many; 19. more; 20. many

Page 39
1. Italian (P), new, bright, red, Irish (P), million, Belgian (P), other, Mexican (P), Greek (P), California (P), Bastille Day (P), Chicago (P), Siamese (P), few, English (P), French (P), several, German (P), Swedish (P), silk, Japanese (P), purple, African (P), English (P), small, Michigan (P), orange, digital; 2. (circled) which (underlined) part; 3. (circled) What (underlined) type; 4. (circled) Which (underlined) system; 5. (circled) What (underlined) brand; 6. (circled) What (underlined) store; Paragraphs will vary.

Page 40
1. (underlined) are, (circled) necessary; 2. (underlined) is, (circled) delicious; 3. (underlined) is, (circled) golden; 4. (underlined) are, (circled) industrious; 5. (underlined) is, (circled) supreme; 6. (underlined) are, (circled) tiny; 7. (underlined) are, (circled) dependent; 8. (underlined) are, (circled) happy; 9. (underlined) are, (circled) tiny; 10. (underlined) are, (circled) unpopular; 11. Paragraphs will vary. 12. Answers will vary. 13. Answers will vary. 14. Answers will vary. 15. Answers will vary.

Page 41
1. (circled) always, (underlined) have, needed; 2. (circled) first, (underlined) came; 3. (circled) then, (underlined) made; 4. (circled) Eventually, (underlined) established; 5. (circled) never, (underlined) could, vote; 6. (circled) Later, (underlined) adapted; 7. (circled) often, (underlined) were; 8. (circled) always, eventually, (underlined) followed; 9. (circled) frequently, (underlined) allow; 10. (circled) Today, (underlined) look; 11. (circled) often, better, (underlined) feel, works; 12. (circled) constantly, (underlined) are, working; 13. (circled) always, (underlined) is; 14. Answers will vary. 15. Answers will vary. 16. Answers will vary. 17. Answers will vary.

Page 42
1. (circled) everywhere, (underlined) have looked; 2. (circled) away, (underlined) stayed; 3. (circled) nearby, (underlined) developed; 4. (circled) there, (underlined) ruled; 5. (circled) here, (underlined) came; 6. (circled) inward, (underlined) focused; 7. (circled) in, (underlined) brought; 8. (circled) outside, (underlined) looked; 9. (circled) out, (underlined) spread; 10. (circled) there, (underlined) look; 11. Answers will vary. 12. Answers will vary. 13. Answers will vary. 14. Answers will vary. 15. Answers will vary.

Page 43
1. (circled) eagerly, (underlined) play; 2. (circled) carefully, (underlined) listen; 3. (circled) completely, (underlined) understand; 4. (circled) carefully, (underlined) must be, controlled; 5. (circled) easily, (underlined) can, be played; 6. (circled) gracefully, (underlined) execute; 7. (circled) emotionally, (underlined) react; 8. (circled) competitively, (underlined) was, played; 9. (circled) passionately, (underlined) were played; 10. (circled) rapidly, (underlined) spread; 11. (circled) avidly, (underlined) watched; 12. (circled) only, (underlined) played; 13. (circled) intensely, (underlined) must be played; 14. (circled) quickly, (underlined) run; 15. (circled) passionately, (underlined) cheer; 16. Answers will vary. 17. Answers will vary. 18. Answers will vary. 19. Answers will vary.

Page 44
1. soon/sooner/soonest; hard/harder/hardest; noisily/more-less noisily/most-least noisily; late/later/latest; easily/more-less easily/most-least easily; efficiently/more-less efficiently/most-least efficiently; loudly/more-less loudly/most-least loudly; proudly/more-less proudly/most-least proudly; harshly/more-less harshly/most-least harshly; neatly/more-less neatly/most-least neatly; cheerfully/more-less cheerfully/most-least cheerfully; courageously/more-less courageously/most-least courageously; highly/more-less highly/most-least highly 2. more quickly, C; 3. fast, P; 4. nearest, S; 5. roughly, P; 6. more carefully, C

Page 45
1. strangely (ADV); 2. sudden (ADJ); 3. calmly (ADV); 4. usual (ADJ); 5. extremely (ADV); 6. Gradually (ADV); 7. wise (ADJ); 8. guilty (ADJ); 9. swiftly (ADV); 10. awkwardly (ADV); 11. poor (ADJ); 12. odd (ADJ); 13. quickly (ADV); 14. thoroughly (ADV); 15. Answers will vary. 16. Answers will vary. 17. Answers will vary. 18. Answers will vary.

Page 46
1. Wow; 2. Great; 3. No; 4. Oh no; 5. Oh; 6. Rats; 7. Zounds; 8. Shh; 9. Yes; 10. Right; 11. Ah; 12. Hey; 13. Surprise; 14. Gosh; 15. Super; 16. Answers will vary. 17. Answers will vary. 18. Answers will vary. 19. Answers will vary.

Page 47
1. and, CO; 2. and, CO; 3. but, CO; 4. neither-nor, CR; 5. if, SU; 6. though, SU; 7. Though, SU; 8. because, SU; 9. but, CO; 10. when, SU; 11. and, CO; 12. not only-but also, CR

Page 48
1. adverb; 2. noun; 3. pronoun; 4. noun; 5. preposition; 6. verb; 7. adjective; 8. adjective; 9. noun; 10. verb; 11. Answers will vary. 12. Answers will vary. 13. Answers will vary. 14. Answers will vary. 15. Answers will vary.

Page 49
1. adverb; 2. verb; 3. pronoun; 4. noun; 5. preposition; 6. adverb; 7. conjunction; 8. pronoun; 9. verb; 10. conjunction; 11. adjective; 12. interjection

Page 50
1. (underlined) my older sister, (circled) Kami; 2. (underlined) a vintage roadster, (circled) car; 3. (underlined) the village chief, (circled) man; 4. (underlined) my favorite sport, (circled) Baseball; 5. (underlined) a Democrat, (circled) senator; 6. (underlined) our Latin teacher, (circled) Mr. Tobias; 7. (underlined) a rambling shack, (circled) house; 8. (underlined) a huge German shepherd, (circled) dog; 9. (underlined) a sleek cruiser, (circled) boat; 10. (underlined) a grey manx, (circled) cat; 11. (underlined) the movie theater, (circled) Studio 28; 12. (underlined) butter pecan, (circled) ice cream; 13. Answers will vary. 14. Answers will vary. 15. Answers will vary. 16. Answers will vary.

Page 51
1. who; 2. whom; 3. who; 4. whom; 5. Who; 6. whom; 7. whom; 8. whom; 9. who; 10. whom; 11. Who; 12. whom; 13. who; 14. Who; Paragraphs will vary.

Page 52
1. "Look out!" Jackie cried. 2. "Didn't you see that broken step?" Jackie asked. 3. "No," Ahmad said. "Thanks for warning me." 4. "I think we should fix that before someone gets hurt," Jackie suggested. 5. "Do you know where there's a hammer?" Ahmad queried. 6. "I don't," Jackie admitted, "but maybe Emily does." 7. "Hey, Emily!" she yelled. "Where's the hammer?" 8. "Don't yell," responded Emily. "I'm right behind you." Answers will vary.

Answer Key

Page 53
1. DQ: Pilar said, "We're going to the Winter Olympics!" 2. DQ: "How are you getting there?" Jaime asked. 3. IQ; 4. DQ: "We're flying," Pilar said, "and I can't wait to go!" 5. IQ; 6. IQ; 7. DQ: "Are you really going to see the figure skating?" Ashton asked. 8. DQ: Pilar said, "Yes, my father has already bought tickets." 9. DQ: "Well, I'd rather see the downhill skiing," Jaime interjected. 10. IQ; 11. IQ; 12. DQ: "May I come along with you?" Demetri implored. 13. Answers will vary. 14. Answers will vary. 15. Answers will vary. 16. Answers will vary.

Page 54
1. "'Chicago' is my favorite poem," Bill said. 2. "That's just because you grew up there," Rick replied. 3. "That's not true," Bill corrected. "I like the way Sandburg writes." 4. "When Bill said, 'I like the way Sandburg writes', I think he really meant it," added Hestor. 5. "Did you do your homework yet?" Benji asked. 6. "I read the chapter 'Tropical Rainforests' in my science book," added Hestor. 7. Ingrid started singing "Auld Lang Syne." 8. The class read "The Seven Stages of Man." 9. Sabena wondered if "Rules of the Game" was included in the book of short stories. 10. The term "short story" is defined in the glossary. 11. Norman wondered what authors the teacher considered "flaky." 12. "What kind of question is that?" asked the teacher. 13. "Is that word in the dictionary?" Alexa inquired. 14. "Did Norman say, 'I'll look that up'?" inquired the teacher.

Page 55
(underlined once, underlined twice) 1. capital, is; 2. it, is; 3. scenery, is; 4. homes, are; 5. home, is; 6. map, is; 7. you, will go; 8. you, have been; 9. rain forests, are; 10. Great Barrier Reef, is; 11. Australia, is; 12. Australia, does trade

Page 56
1. (underlined) person, (circled) mineralogist (PN); 2. (underlined) Minerals, (circled) useful (PA); 3. (underlined) Minerals, (circled) ore minerals (PN); 4. (underlined) minerals, (circled) beautiful (PA); 5. (underlined) emeralds, (circled) green (PA); 6. (underlined) mineral, (circled) diamond (PN); 7. (underlined) diamond, (circled) it (PPN); 8. (underlined) mineral, (circled) harder (PA); 9. (underlined) Graphite, (circled) soft (PA); 10. (underlined) substance, (circled) it (PPN); 11. (underlined) property, (circled) specific gravity (PN); 12. (underlined) gold ore, (circled) heavy (PA); 13. (underlined) hobby, (circled) popular (PA); 14. (underlined) obtaining certain minerals, (circled) challenge (PN); 15. (underlined) minerals, (circled) materials (PN)

Page 57
1. (circled) won, (underlined) championship; 2. (circled) answered, (underlined) question; 3. (circled) boarded, (underlined) train; 4. (circled) sold, (underlined) shirt; 5. (circled) sent, (underlined) troops; 6. (circled) read, (underlined) newspaper; 7. (circled) sent, (underlined) reporters; 8. (circled) gave, (underlined) check; 9. (circled) grabbed, (underlined) basketball; 10. (circled) wants, return, (underlined) us, car; 11. (circled) sponsors, (underlined) Honor Society; 12. (circled) joined, (underlined) team; 13. (circled) won, (underlined) prize; 14. (circled) threw, (underlined) balloon; 15. Answers will vary. 16. Answers will vary.

Page 58
1. (circled) told, (underlined) him; 2. (circled) taught, (underlined) choir; 3. (circled) gave, (underlined) Shannon; 4. (circled) sent, (underlined) Bailey; 5. (circled) fed, (underlined) geese; 6. (circled) left, (underlined) me; 7. (circled) handed, (underlined) employee; 8. (circled) won, (underlined) her; 9. (circled) offered, (underlined) clients; 10. (circled) offered, (underlined) secretary; 11. (circled) gave, (underlined) them; 12. Answers will vary. 13. Answers will vary. 14. Answers will vary.

Page 59
1. (underlined) on Thanksgiving Day, (circled) Thanksgiving Day; 2. (underlined) from her home, (circled) home; 3. (underlined) into her bedroom, (circled) bedroom; 4. (underlined) for Tyesha, in the car, (circled) Tyesha, car; 5. (underlined) under her bed, (circled) bed; 6. (underlined) by the bed, (circled) bed; 7. (underlined) in the kitchen, (circled) kitchen; 8. (underlined) in the phone book, (circled) phone book; 9. (underlined) in the refrigerator, (circled) refrigerator; 10. (underlined) at our house, (circled) house; 11. (underlined) into the driveway, (circled) driveway; 12. Answers will vary. 13. Answers will vary. 14. Answers will vary.

Page 60
1. (underlined) in the news, (circled) People; 2. (underlined) in town, (circled) drugstore; 3. (underlined) with the best choreography, (circled) musical; 4. (underlined) in a red jumpsuit, in a chiffon dress, (circled) gorilla, chimpanzee; 5. (underlined) beside the gurgling brook, (circled) cottage; 6. (underlined) of students' addresses, (circled) list; 7. (underlined) in this class, (circled) Nobody; 8. (underlined) in this hospital, (circled) doctors; 9. (underlined) to the safe, (circled) combination; 10. (underlined) on the computer, (circled) graphics; 11. Answers will vary. 12. Answers will vary. 13. Answers will vary. 14. Answers will vary. 15. Answers will vary. 16. Answers will vary. 17. Answers will vary.

Page 61
1. (underlined) under the students' weight, (circled) sagged; 2. (underlined) into the puddle, (circled) fell; 3. (underlined) over the hurdle, (circled) jumped; 4. (underlined) with care, under the tree, (circled) wrapped, placed; 5. (underlined) under the bridge, (circled) walked; 6. (underlined) from the plane, (circled) pushed; 7. (underlined) into the forest, (circled) rushed; 8. (underlined) after the defeat, through the night, (circled) traveled; 9. (underlined) behind the barn, (circled) sitting; 10. (underlined) in their buggies, (circled) travel; 11. (underlined) into the tree, (circled) flew; 12. (underlined) with graceful movements, (circled) danced; 13. (underlined) around the clouds, (circled) flashes; 14. (underlined) with shocking speed, (circled) moves; 15. Answers will vary. 16. Answers will vary. 17. Answers will vary.

Page 62
1. OK; 2. Answers will vary. 3. OK; 4. Answers will vary. 5. OK; 6. OK; 7. Answers will vary. 8. OK; 9. Answers will vary. 10. OK

Page 63
1. S; 2. S; 3. F; 4. F; 5. S; 6. F; 7. S; 8. S; 9. F; 10. S; 11. F; 12. S; 13. S; 14. S; 15. Answers will vary. 16. Answers will vary.

Page 64
1. Answers will vary. 2. Answers will vary. 3. Answers will vary. 4. Answers will vary. 5. Answers will vary. 6. Answers will vary.

Page 65
1. Studying leaves is fascinating. There are so many different kinds. 2. Leaves come in different shades of green; no two kinds seem to be the same. 3. Leaves that grow in low light are usually dark green; leaves that grow in bright light are lighter green. 4. A leaf's shape is important. Experts can tell a lot about a tree from the shape of its leaves. 5. Leaves from rain forest plants often have drip tips; these are pointed tips that

Answer Key

help water run off the leaf. 6. Some leaves have complicated shapes. These shapes allow the wind to blow the leave without tearing it.

Page 66

1. The moray eel conceals himself by hiding in the rocks; he pops his head out to catch his prey. 2. A group of sea animals shoots water through one of two body openings, so they are named sea squirts. 3. Starfish and sea urchins have no heads, so they have mouths on their bellies. 4. Starfish have five flexible arms; they use them to walk around. 5. A seahorse is a fish that swims in an upright position. The male has a kangaroo-like pouch that holds the fertilized eggs until they hatch. 6. Most sea urchins are vegetarians or scavengers, and most are equipped with five sharp teeth for scraping food. 7. Sand dollars are shallow-water echnioderms. Their bodies are covered with spines that aid in locomotion. 8. Seaweed is commonly found along rocky beaches; it grows attached to the rocks. 9. Female sea turtles come ashore to lay their eggs in holes; they dig the holes and then cover them with sand. 10. A sea otter's hind feet are broadened into flippers; his forefeet are useful for grasping. 11. The sea cucumber is a type of sea animal with a long, fleshy body. It belongs to the echinoderm group. 12. Gulls are long-winged birds. They are often seen flying and dipping over large bodies of water. 13. Scientists still don't even know all the basic facts about famous sea life. The habits of great white sharks have been puzzling them for years. 14. Many people are afraid of sharks, but some people are not. 15. Aquariums are places that try to teach people about fish and marine life. An aquarium's tanks are very difficult to maintain. 16. Educating people about sea life is the job of a marine biologist; this is a highly specialized field of study.

Page 67

(underlined once, underlined twice) 1. bird, is named; 2. food, is; 3. nests, are; 4. bird, enlists; 5. ally, is; 6. ratel, is called; 7. honey, is; 8. skin, resists; 9. bird, finds; 10. It, chatters; 11. bird, leads; 12. ratel, breaks; 13. animal, eats; 14. bird, eats

Page 68

(underlined once, underlined twice) 1. The people in many parts of the world, are unable to feed themselves in times of disaster. 2. International relief agencies and many governments, send aid to those people. 3. The most famous international relief agency, is the Red Cross. 4. The Red Cross, was founded in 1864 to aid victims of war. 5. Red Cross workers, fight misery in times of both war and peace. 6. Over 135 nations, have Red Cross societies. 7. Each Red Cross society, runs its own program. 8. The American Red Cross, has more than 10 million volunteers. 9. Voluntary contributions, fund the programs and services of the American Red Cross. 10. All aid to disaster victims, is free. 11. Answers will vary.

Page 69

1. Answers will vary. 2. Answers will vary. 3. Answers will vary. 4. Answers will vary. 5. Answers will vary. 6. Answers will vary. 7. Answers will vary. 8. Answers will vary.

Page 70

1. is; 2. heats; 3. creates; 4. are; 5. suffer; 6. have; 7. provide; 8. is; 9. think; 10. is; 11. Answers will vary.

Page 71

1. (circled) We, (underlined) it; 2. (circled) he, (underlined) it; 3. (underlined) it; 4. (circled) They, (underlined) us; 5. (circled) I; 6. (circled) I, (underlined) her; 7. (circled) She; 8. (underlined) it; 9. (circled) They; 10. (circled) He, (underlined) them;

11. (underlined) me; 12. (circled) We, (underlined) it; 13. Answers will vary.

Page 72

(underlined once, underlined twice) 1. I'm going south, When the cold weather arrives; 2. The class really enjoyed the movie, that showed life under the sea. 3. raise your hand, If you think you know the answer; 4. I was about to leave for my vacation, when I noticed that the tire was flat. 5. Felipe really liked the car, that we bought for him at the auction. 6. Trisha was really disappointed, that we could not go. 7. it was not easy for him, Until history became Henry's favorite subject; 8. we're going to race each other, When David builds a new radio-controlled car; 9. that we had purchased. 10. please call the doctor, If the pain does not go away; 11. Sheila knows many people, who can play bridge. 12. Tia thought she knew just how he felt, because she'd had the same experience. 13. I have not yet heard the song, that the popular singer recorded in Finnish. 14. The paramedics grabbed the oxygen, when they saw the patient turning blue. 15. You have not lived, until you take a trip down the Colorado River in a raft. 16. he had already left, When I returned to the store

Page 73

1. (underlined) who gave you the detention, (circled) teacher; 2. (underlined) that seem to have disappeared, (circled) traditions; 3. (underlined) that was used before, (circled) color; 4. (underlined) that Iesha most enjoyed, (circled) activity; 5. (underlined) that was in the front window, (circled) desk; 6. (underlined) that had been freshly painted, (circled) table; 7. (underlined) who applied for the job, (circled) person; 8. (underlined) whose gun fell from his holster, (circled) officer; 9. (underlined) where they caught all of the fish, (circled) lake; 10. (underlined) that we visited, (circled) city; 11. (underlined) to which the critic referred, (circled) play; 12. (underlined) that I liked, (circled) horse; 13. (underlined) who might help us, (circled) students; 14. (underlined) that faces south, (circled) wall; 15. Answers will vary. 16. Answers will vary. 17. Answers will vary. 18. Answers will vary.

Page 74

1. (underlined) which are used to catch prey, (circled) claws; 2. (underlined) which are called talons, (circled) claws; 3. (underlined) that have fingerprints much like a human's, (circled) fingers; 4. (underlined) that is slippery, (circled) prey; 5. (underlined) which all have long, sharp claws, (circled) fingers and toes; 6. (underlined) who must learn to hunt, (circled) cubs; 7. (underlined) which has no claws, (circled) hoof; 8. (underlined) which hunts fish swimming near the water's surface, (circled) fishing bat; 9. (underlined) that she will use to protect her eggs, (circled) hole; 10. (underlined) that point forward, that point backward, (circled) toes, toes; 11. (underlined) that are often dug by the wolves' parents, (circled) dens; 12. (underlined) that are found on the feet of birds, reptiles, and mammals, (circled) claws; 13. (underlined) which grow long, (circled) toenails; 14. (underlined) which is hardened cells of the epidermis, the outer layer of skin, (circled) material

Page 75

1. when the teacher speaks (when); 2. Because I read the book (why); 3. before he began the surgery (when); 4. when Jay entered the room (when); 5. because it is the best (why); 6. Because you have been so nice (why); 7. Before Jessi started running (when); 8. where the backpack was last seen (where); 9. by moving my arms (how); 10. After the class is over (when); 11. When you get to the light (when); 12. because she wanted

Answer Key

to join the team (why); 13. Since the book was about dogs (why); 14. Answers will vary. 15. Answers will vary. 16. Answers will vary. 17. Answers will vary.

Page 76
1. That you should eat your vegetables (S); 2. What Heather did today (S); 3. that rain was expected (DO); 4. whatever time you designate (OP); 5. what I would like to see today (PN); 6. whomever comes to the door (IO); 7. Whose books these are (S); 8. whoever completes the course (OP or IO); 9. what you make it (PN); 10. What you say (S); 11. How a computer works (S); 12. Whoever wrote this graffiti (S); 13. what the minor league players craved (PN); 14. that this plan will work (DO); Answers will vary.

Page 77
1. what they could do to earn money (DO); 2. that her idea might work (DO); 3. What Felicia proposed (S); 4. That people would want their windows cleaned (S); 5. How to get the proper equipment (S); 6. whatever they could promise (S); 7. whoever called in the first week (IO); 8. that the fliers should be hand-delivered (DO); 9. what they expected (PN); 10. Whoever had the dirtiest windows (S); 11. That you should keep your word (S); 12. whomever called (IO); 13. whomever they could (OP)

Page 78
1. whoever would listen (N); 2. How you play the game (N); 3. that is considered soothing (ADJ); 4. so that we can go together (ADV); 5. what his real problem is (N); 6. that hit the town (ADJ); 7. when he is at the ball park (ADV); 8. until she could barely move (ADV); 9. that he had stolen the idea for the movie (N); 10. which is one of the Great Lakes (ADJ); 11. that we couldn't go to the play (N); 12. Answers will vary. 13. Answers will vary. 14. Answers will vary.

Page 79
1. that was like all the others (ADJ); 2. before winter ends (ADV); 3. that no one would forget (ADJ); 4. What Craig thought of (N); 5. What we would do(N); 6. because the snow packed so well (ADV); 7. who lives next door (ADJ); 8. What became the monster's body (N); 9. after we hoisted the second ball on top of the first (ADV); 10. To build his height (ADV); 11. Since we were building a giant snow monster (ADV); 12. When the mound of snow was big enough (ADV); 13. When we stood back and looked (ADV); 14. What he needed (N); 15. by spraying him with colored water; (ADV); 16. that we put so much hard work into (ADJ); 17. that lives down the street (ADJ); 18. when we saw his startled expression (ADV) ; 19. That our snow monster was unusual (N); 20. that we had so much fun (ADJ)

Page 80
1. (underlined) what make holidays delicious, PN; 2. (underlined) Whoever made this chocolate pie, S; 3. (underlined) that this caramel corn isn't stale, DO; 4. (underlined) whoever says "please", IO; 5. (underlined) after how much they ate, OP; 6. (underlined) who drives the ice-cream truck (circled) man; 7. (underlined) that the bees make (circled) honey; 8. (underlined) which was the size of a golf ball (circled) jawbreaker; 9. (underlined) where my cousin works (circled) bakery; 10. (underlined) who worked in town (circled) fudge maker; 11. whenever you've eaten sweets (when);12. because he ate too much candy (why);13. As winter progresses (when); 14. by dipping strawberries in melted chocolate (how); 15. that opened recently (where)

Page 81
1. S; 2. C; 3. S; 4. S; 5. S; 6. C; 7. C; 8. S; 9. C; 10. C; 11. S; 12. C

Page 82
1. C: (underlined) Chartres Cathedral, it, (circled) is, has become; 2. S: (underlined) town, (circled) is built; 3. C: (underlined) Chartres, it, (circled) is located, is; 4. S: (underlined) cathedral, (circled) has; 5. C: (underlined) Cathedrals, people, (circled) were, devoted; 6. C: (underlined) fire, it, (circled) destroyed, was rebuilt; 7. Answers will vary. 8. Answers will vary.

Page 83
(underlined once, underlined twice) 1. The astronauts left the vehicle, when the solar panel failed. 2. The United States became serious about space exploration, when the Soviet Union launched *Sputnik I*. 3. humans have not succeeded in finding it, If there is life on the moon; 4. many people share the credit, When a spacecraft is put in orbit; 5. Yuri Gagarin died in 1968, who was the first person to orbit the earth; 6. The Apollo program had a lunar module, that was capable of landing on the moon and returning to the main vehicle. 7. The *Sputnik I* was the first artificial satellite, which was launched in 1957; 8. he was fulfilling a promise made by America's President Kennedy earlier in the decade, When Neil Armstrong stepped onto the lunar surface; 9. The United States launched the space shuttle *Columbia*, which was the first reusable manned spacecraft. 10. The *Challenger* exploded in midair, which had seven astronauts on board; 11. all American missions were temporarily stopped, Because this disaster was so devastating; 12. Answers will vary. 13. Answers will vary. 14. Answers will vary.

Page 84
(underlined once, underlined twice) 1. let us know, we will try it; If you have a solution; 2. she was able to play brilliantly, she beat Samia soundly; Because Torika had studied previous chess matches; 3. Austin will put up the tent, Carla will start the fire; When we get to the park; 4. Jeremy cut it, Isabella ate it; Though the steak was not fully cooked; 5. Wallace had never gone to college, he worked at the factory; until he won a scholarship. 6. The food was free, the people enjoyed it; who came; 7. the stereo would not play, it destroyed my tape; Though it was brand new; 8. she could not play in the concert, the orchestra sounded terrible; Because Jennifer broke her arm; 9. Paige suggested the movie, Elijah and Michael agreed; when they heard her choice. 10. Stephen went back to Florida, it was not a financial success; where he opened a law firm; 11. The enraged investor sued the company, he was deeply in debt; when he finally won his case; 12. Answers will vary. 13. Answers will vary. 14. Answers will vary.

Page 85
1. C; 2. S; 3. CX; 4. S; 5. C/CX; 6. CX; 7. S; 8. C/CX; 9. S; 10. C; 11. CX; 12. C/CX; 13. S; 14. C/CX; 15. CX; 16 C; 17. S; 18. CX

Page 86
1. C/CX; 2. C; 3. C/CX; 4. CX; 5. C/CX; 6. S; 7. C; 8. C; 9. C; 10. C; 11. C; 12. S; 13. C; 14. C/CX

Page 87
(underlined; circled) 1. small; very fast; 2. huge; gray; eagerly; 3. talented; gracefully; 4. distraught; silently; 5. excited; with the dog; 6. long-stemmed; in a tangled mess, on the floor; 7. frightened, in the window; wildly; 8. Answers will vary. 9. Answers will vary. 10. Answers will vary. 11. Answers will vary. 12. Answers will vary. 13. Answers will vary. 14. Answers will vary. 15. Answers will vary. 16. Answers will vary. 17. Answers will vary.

Page 88
1. Answers will vary. (original misplaced modifier: After school) 2. Answers will vary. (original misplaced modifier: Under the flowerpot) 3. Answers will vary. (original misplaced modifier:

Answer Key

unfortunately) 4. Answers will vary. (original misplaced modifier: to let myself in) 5. Answers will vary. (original misplaced modifier: On the roof) 6. Answers will vary. (original misplaced modifier: for an hour) 7. Answers will vary. (original misplaced modifier: when she arrives) 8. Answers will vary. (original misplaced modifier: through the window)

Page 89
1. While running down to the water; 2. Surrounded by a moat, or OK; 3. OK; 4. Reclining on the beach; 5. OK; 6. Answers will vary. 7. Answers will vary. 8. Answers will vary. 9. Answers will vary. 10. Answers will vary.

Page 90
1. on Monday, Answers will vary. 2. that raced past, Answers will vary. 3. that needed more space, Answers will vary. 4. of boating accidents, Answers will vary. 5. Chilled by the snow; 6. OK; 7. Living on the beach all summer; 8. Startled by the wild animal

Page 91
1. haven't, no, Answers will vary. 2. don't, nothing, Answers will vary. 3. can't, hardly, Answers will vary. 4. didn't, no one, Answers will vary. 5. couldn't, hardly, Answers will vary. 6. doesn't, nothing, Answers will vary. 7. hasn't, never, Answers will vary. 8. would not, no, Answers will vary. 9. didn't, nowhere, Answers will vary.

Page 92
1. Answers will vary. 2. Answers will vary. 3. Answers will vary. 4. Answers will vary. 5. Answers will vary. 6. Answers will vary. 7. Answers will vary. 8. Answers will vary.

Page 93
Paragraphs will vary.

Page 94
1. lay; 2. laid; 3. lay; 4. lies; 5. laid; 6. lay; 7. lie; 8. Lay; 9. laid; 10. Answers will vary. 11. Answers will vary. 12. Answers will vary.

Page 95
1. sat; 2. sit; 3. sit; 4. set; 5. sat; 6. set; 7. sit; 8. sit; 9. sat; 10. Answers will vary. 11. Answers will vary. 12. Answers will vary.

Page 96
1. rises; 2. rose; 3. rise; 4. raised; 5. rose; 6. raised; 7. raised; 8. raised; 9. Answers will vary. 10. Answers will vary. 11. Answers will vary. 12. Answers will vary.

Page 97
Chart, second column: led, ate, wore, blew; third column: frozen, known, caught; 1. blew; 2. eaten; 3. wear; 4. shook; 5. knew; 6. drowned; 7. led; 8. frozen; 9. caught; 10. worn; 11. frozen; 12. Answers will vary. 13. Answers will vary. 14. Answers will vary.

Page 98
Chart, second column: drank, flowed, swore, climbed; third column: chosen, thrown, written, seen; 1. sworn; 2. flowed; 3. wrote; 4. became; 5. has; 6. saw; 7. chosen; 8. drank; 9. thrown; 10. swore; 11. become; 12. flowed; 13. Answers will vary. 14. Answers will vary.

Page 99
Chart, second column: dragged, wove, took, went; third column: wrung, lent, said, let; 1. woven; 2. lent; 3. said; 4. taken; 5. wrung; 6. went; 7. cut; 8. gone; 9. dragged; 10. Answers will vary. 11. Answers will vary. 12. Answers will vary. 13. Answers will vary. 14. Answers will vary.

Page 100
1. Whose; 2. already; 3. all together; 4. there; 5. than; 6. It's;

7. Who's; 8. all ready; 9. altogether; 10. Their; 11. then; 12. They're; 13. It's; 14. its; 15. already; 16. than

Page 101
1. brake; 2. later; 3. lead; 4. loose; 5. principal; 6. led; 7. lose; 8. principle; 9. break; 10. latter; 11. plane; 12. plain; 13. later; 14. principles; 15. plane

Page 102
1. (underlined) sleeping, (circled) child; 2. (underlined) surging, (circled) river; 3. (underlined) singing, (circled) voice; 4. (underlined) dried, (circled) flowers; 5. (underlined) satisfied, (circled) customers; 6. (underlined) wrecked, (circled) cars; 7. (underlined) watched, (circled) pot; 8. (underlined) shaking, (circled) knees; 9. (underlined) Opening the door, (circled) Greg; 10. (underlined) pictured in the brochure, (circled) car; 11. (underlined) eating leaves, (circled) giraffe; 12. (underlined) Breathing hard, (circled) runner; 13. (underlined) knocking loudly on the door, (circled) police; 14. (underlined) Entering the store, (circled) Evelyn; 15. (underlined) Slipping into the water, (circled) diver

Page 103
1. about their moping son, P; 2. Discovering Rosaline's name on the guest list, P; 3. Wearing a mask, P; 4. smiling, P; 5. dancing, P; 6. Struck by love, PA; 7. feuding, P; 8. Appearing on the balcony, P; 9. Overheard by Romeo, PA; 10. determined, PA; 11. Standing before the friar, P; 12. Committed to being reunited, PA; 13. Deceived by his sleeping wife, PA; 14. awakening, P

Page 104
1. to ski, DO; 2. To fish, S; 3. to play, DO; 4. to go, DO; 5. To debate, S; 6. To sleep, S; 7. to vote, PN; 8. to speak, DO; 9. to communicate, PN; 10. to raise one thousand dollars, PN; 11. to pass the class with ease, DO; 12. to go to the game by himself, DO; 13. To finish this paper by tomorrow, S; 14. to make the trip alone, DO; 15. To win a championship, S; 16. to rescue the boy, DO; 17. to show us several ways of solving the problem, DO; 18. to have it all, DO

Page 105
1. Exercising, S; 2. skiing, PN; 3. painting, DO; 4. skating, DO; 5. tolling, S; 6. Whispering, S; 7. practicing, OP; 8. Jogging, S; 9. reading her book, OP; 10. reading historical novels, DO; 11. Flipping hamburgers, S; 12. introducing the players to one another, OP; 13. Drinking a lot of water, S; 14. collecting newspapers to recycle, PN; 15. Asking questions, S; 16. Playing baseball, S

Page 106
1. Cleaning, S; 2. cooking, DO; 3. complaining, OP; 4. procrastinating, PN; 5. Vacuuming, S; 6. dusting, DO; 7. washing, DO; 8. Mopping, S; 9. making, DO; 10. Mowing the lawn, S; 11. pulling weeds, OP; 12. Washing dishes, S; 13. scrubbing the toilet, PN; 14. polishing the silver, OP; 15. Feeding the cat, S; 16. folding laundry, OP; 17. fixing things, PN; 18. finishing the job, PN

Page 107
1. to buy some fresh vegetables, I; 2. Known as one of the best pitchers in baseball, P; 3. juggling three apples at a time, G; 4. to study on a regular basis, I; 5. to exercise every day, I; 6. Talking to himself, G; 7. to have everybody over for dinner, I; 8. Taking a vitamin, G; 9. Standing up to his knees in the water, G; 10. to go to the amusement park, I; 11. Exhausted from the long journey, P; 12. Hooking rugs, G; 13. depressed by the poor attendance, P; 14. Baking cookies, G; 15. painting seashells, G; 16. Answers will vary. 17. Answers will vary. 18. Answers will vary.

Answer Key

Page 108

(underlined once, underlined twice) 1. Amelia Earhart, flew; 2. She, made; 3. Amelia, opened; 4. Ms. Earhart, worked; 5. She earned; 6. She, married; 7. pilot, tried; 8. plane, disappeared; 9. disappearance, fueled; 10. people, believe; 11. navigator, vanished; 12. Answers will vary. 13. Answers will vary. 14. Answers will vary. 15. Answers will vary. 16. Answers will vary.

Page 109

take, must sit, provide, will grow, form, develop, cover, forms, allow, lies, pushes, uses, dries, fluffs, begins, ranges, cover, will keep, come, develop, help keep, help, vary

Page 110

1. Answers will vary. 2. Answers will vary. 3. Answers will vary. 4. Answers will vary. 5. Answers will vary. 6. Answers will vary. 7. Answers will vary. 8. Answers will vary. 9. Answers will vary.

Page 111

1. is eaten, Answers will vary. 2. are enjoyed, Answers will vary. 3. is enjoyed, Answers will vary. 4. are favored, Answers will vary. 5. is served, Answers will vary. 6. has been made, Answers will vary.

Page 112

1. P, Answers will vary. 2. P, Answers will vary. 3. A; 4. A; 5. P, Answers will vary. 6. P, Answers will vary. 7. A

Page 113

1. A; 2. P, Answers will vary. 3. A; 4. A; 5. P, Answers will vary. 6. A; 7. P, Answers will vary. 8. P, Answers will vary. 9. A

Page 114

1. Answers will vary. 2. Answers will vary. 3. Answers will vary. 4. Answers will vary. 5. Answers will vary. 6. Answers will vary. 7. Answers will vary. 8. Answers will vary. 9. Answers will vary. 10. Answers will vary. 11. Answers will vary. 12. Answers will vary. 13. Answers will vary. 14. (blank) 15. I; 16. (blank) 17. I; 18. (blank); 19. (blank)

Page 115

1. Y; 2. Y; 3. N; 4. N; 5. Y; 6. N; 7. Y; 8. N; 9. Y; 10. Y; 11. N; 12. Y; 13. Answers will vary. 14. Answers will vary. 15. Answers will vary.

Page 116

1. During the Middle Ages,; 2. At that time in European history,; 3. In return for his loyalty,; 4. Under the feudal system,; 5. When a person controlled land,; 6. At the age of about seven,; 7. As soon as a squire had mastered the necessary skills,; 8. As a knight,; 9. Because they had few rights,; 10. In return for clerical services,; 11. Answers will vary. 12. Answers will vary. 13. Answers will vary. 14. Answers will vary. 15. Answers will vary.

Page 117

1. When I graduate from high school, I plan to go to college. 2. Yes, that is a good idea. 3. Of course, you will need good grades to get into the college of your choice. 4. Seeing that you are a good student, I know you'll have no problem. 5. In addition, your involvement in extracurricular activities is important. 6. Travis, what will you be studying in college? 7. If I get there, I'd like to study oceanography. 8. Well, you will have your work cut out for you. 9. You will find, I'm sure, that it is a competitive field. 10. Indeed, it won't be easy. 11. Jack, how about you? 12. I would like, I think, to go to medical school. 13. Fortunately, I've been studying hard all year.

Page 118

1. Hi, call me when you get home. I will, I think, be home all evening. 2. Greg, this is cousin Hugo. We miss you! In addition to that, I have something exciting to tell you. 3. Since you're not home yet, I think I'll go shopping without you. By the way, I did find your bracelet. It was on the counter next to the sink. If you can't come get it, I will put it in the mail. 4. Mom, I went to Scott's. Yes, I already did all of my English homework. I will be home for dinner, of course, especially since it's spaghetti night. 5. Laura, I received your request. For more information, please write to us at the Venezuela Tourist Association. 6. Hello, is this the Lewis residence? Your dog, I believe, is running loose on Jasper Court. If we can, we will lure him into our backyard to keep him safe until you're back. 7. Don't forget your dentist appointment, Mr. Dolby, at 11:00 tomorrow morning. If you can't make it, please call and cancel as soon as possible. 8. This is Rebecca, your niece, calling at 5:00 pm. If you still need a babysitter for Friday night, I can do it. Just give me a call, I guess, whenever you get home. 9. This is Mom, calling to remind you to take out the trash before it gets dark. Oh, and don't forget to brush your teeth before you go to bed. 10. I'm calling on behalf of the Cristoffer Foundation, which is a non-profit organization that helps children in need. Please, don't forget us this year. As you know, our children are counting on you.

Page 119

1. G; 2. J; 3. A; 4. F; 5. B; 6. H; 7. C; 8. D; 9. E; 10. I; 11. T; 12. O; 13. R; 14. S; 15. K; 16. P; 17. L; 18. Q; 19. M; 20. N; 21. Answers will vary. 22. Answers will vary. 23. Answers will vary. 24. Answers will vary. 25. Answers will vary.

Page 120

1. driver; 2. adulthood; 3. neighborhood; 4. freedom; 5. stillness; 6. sickness; 7. government; 8. attendance; 9. kingdom; 10. parenthood; 11. firmness; 12. happiness; 13. amusement; 14. boredom; 15. singer; 16. encouragement; 17. -hood, Answers will vary. 18. -ance, Answers will vary. 19. -er, Answers will vary. 20. -or, Answers will vary. 21. -ment, Answers will vary.